Creating Your Care Plan:
A How-To Guide to Self-Directed Assessments & Getting Your Care Package Right the First Time.

Creating Your Care Plan:
A Comprehensive Guide to Self-Directed Assessments

Copyright © 2025 by Patricia Guthrie
Published in the United Kingdom by Vektor Publishing

First ABCDE Press Edition, 2025 (First Printing)

"All rights reserved. No part of this publication may be reproduced in any form, or by any means, electronic or mechanical, including photocopying, recording, or any information browsing, storage, or retrieval system, without permission in writing from the publisher."

British Library, Boston Spa, Wetherby, West Yorkshire, LS23 7BY:
Guthrie, Patricia.
ISBN 978-1-83709-173-7

Table of Contents

Ch. 1: Understanding Self- Directed Assessments　　5

Ch. 2: Navigating the Self-Directed Assessment Process　　28

Ch. 3: Finding the Right Home Care and Support Worker　　75

Ch. 4: Specialised Home Care for Elderly Patients　　84

Ch. 5: Assessing Individual Needs for Home Care Services　　95

Ch. 6: Resources for Families Seeking Home Care　　118

Ch. 7: Creating a Care Plan　　134

Ch. 8: Evaluating and Interviewing Home Care Workers　　158

Ch. 9: Financial Assistance and Funding Options　　169

Ch. 10: Understanding Patient Rights in Home Care　　186

Ch. 11: Transitioning from Hospital to Home　　194

Ch. 12: Supporting Mental Health During Recovery　　204

Why Does Care Matter?

Life changes quickly, and we have to change and adapt as we move through our individual journeys, as carers and people being care for, we need to learn how to roll with the punches and be prepared to live the best life possible,

Nowadays you don't have to wait until a life altering illness changes how you operate and cope from day to day. Needing help is not unusual. Millions of people in the UK require care.

Approximately 500,000 adults live in care homes. Around 441,479 are elderly individuals, but approximately 20% of care home residents in England are under 65 years of age, with many residents receiving care due to disabilities or long-term health conditions.

There are approximately 4.7 million unpaid carers in England and approximately 310,000 unpaid carers in Wales;

Around 820,000 people receive domiciliary care in the UK. Domiciliary care providers include 'hourly' or 'visiting' home care, supported living, assisted living, or live-in care. These include patients who are ill, elderly, have long-term medical issues, or have been discharged from hospital care.

Around 100,000 people receive long-term support

living, or assisted living care. About 10,000 people need Live-in care.

In August 2024, around 400,000 people were awaiting assessment, review, or the start of a care service. Hospital discharges and assessments continue to be the biggest source of this care backlog and since 2019 the more people are leaving hospitals with more complex care needs.

If you live in the UK, you are hundreds of times more likely to need home care, then to have a car accident. Planning your hospital discharge strategy and planning for home care is just as important as any other insurance plan you can make for your life. If you already receive care, a review of you care plan could be beneficial, whether you, or the person you care for, need recovery, long-term or palliative care. Many people find domiciliary care to be a convenient option, many apply for a local authority care assessment because either they can't afford the cost of living in a care home. Other reasons for considering home care include long waiting lists for community care and care homes, patients trying to avoid discharge delays and need to free up NHS hospital beds. Good home care is expensive, and well sought after. Sometimes the right care may be hard to obtain. This guide is meant to help care users and their carers to understand the care system and the assessment process and learn how to optimise their care package and find and apply for the different types of help, support and funding that may be available.

Chapter 1: Understanding Self-Directed Assessments

Finding good care isn't always easy. The right support should feel comfortable. That's why having **A Good Care Plan Matters**. Care is not just something to think about in crisis; it's something to prepare for before life takes an unexpected turn. Nobody plans for an injury, illness, or disability to disrupt their world, but when it does, having an organised, well-thought-out care plan can mean the difference between scrambling for help and having a clear path for moving forward. Navigating the options, costs, and quality can be overwhelming and making preparations now can save a lot of stress later. Having a care plan should sound like security.

This chapter will give you an overview of Self-Directed Assessments. The Self-Directed process puts you in control of your care, and gives you the flexibility to arrange for the support that fits your lifestyle and preferences. This chapter will also touch on how an Advance Statement or Lasting Power of Attorney (LPA) can help you to pre-plan and prepare for your care.

What is a Self-Directed Assessment?
A Self-Directed Assessment is a process that allows the **Care User** to assess their care needs and decide how their care and support package is arranged, instead of the local authority. This specific type of assessment, which is a powerful tool that is designed to empower potential care clients in managing their care needs after a hospital discharge or during short term or long term periods of incapacity, due to mental or physical disability, injury or chronic illness. Drafting your own care plan is an important part of the social care process, particularly for people who need help with daily tasks and who are managing a long-term illness or disability.

Through a Self-Directed Assessment, individuals can:
Create their own care plan based on their personal needs. Choose their own carers; decide how and where they receive support; Make decisions about how and who receives payment for their care, including options for using Direct Payments, or a Direct Payment Card.

Since Self-Directed Assessments allows clients to

decide on their own care requirements in a structured manner, this approach can lead to a more personalised care. The Self-Directed assessment process gives you an opportunity to articulate your unique needs, your preferences, your wellness goals, and ensures that the support you receive aligns with your lifestyle and choices. Taking charge of your assessment means you are advocating for yourself and paving the way for a more effective and fulfilling care experience.

Requesting a Self-Directed assessment typically involves reaching out to your local authority Adult Social Services department, GP or NHS care provider. It is important to familiarise yourself with the specific procedures for your area, as these can vary. When you initiate the Self-Directed process, be prepared to advocate for yourself, as well as discuss your health condition, daily activities, and any challenges you face.

Providing detailed and precise information on your care needs is crucial, as the data will inform the assessment team about the level and type of support you require and helps with any appeal. Remember, the assessment will be your opportunity to express your needs openly, and the more details you provide, the better your care package will be.

The conventional care needs assessment is typically where the local authority is contacted regarding a funded care package and then someone from the council such as a social worker or occupational therapist visits you at your home and asks you how you're managing everyday tasks like washing, dressing and cooking. They might ask you to describe how well you do certain things like making a cup of tea and getting out of a chair. This assessment is supposed to cover all key issues for your care plan, but the person doing the assessment can only make notes about 'presenting needs' – meaning, only the needs that are mentioned during the needs assessment itself are taken into account. If they forget to ask you about something important and you don't bring it up, it simply won't be included in your care plan. People often downplay their real day-to-day difficulties in their assessment. This often affects the level of support they get.

A Self-Directed care plan will be supported by social service staff, but it is a tool for the care user to decide what type of care they need and how their care will be provided, because it allows the care client to take a direct approach to social care and to have much greater control over their funded care package. The way self-directed client manage their independent care plan; usually works by the care user being allocated a combination of direct payments, payment cards, and individual budgets, and employing a mix of council commission care agencies and private carers. They are then able to get the best care possible, by making sure that before their self-directed assessment there is complete list made of every issue and challenge they are facing, to ensure nothing is forgotten.

If you choose to self-direct, once your assessment process is underway, it's essential to carefully consider the type of home care and, or support worker that will best meet your needs. You will need people who are not only qualified but also have a temperament and approach that resonates with you. This could mean finding someone with experience in dealing with your specific health condition, or simply someone whose personality makes you feel comfortable.

Interviewing potential carers can be a vital step in the Self-Directed Assessment process, allowing you to gauge their experience, skills, and compatibility with your personality and healthcare philosophy.

Navigating through the Self-Directed assessment process and overseeing the subsequent care arrangements is a daunting task, but there are numerous resources available to support you. Many of the organisations listed below provide guidance on evaluating home care options and they can even assist in connecting you with reputable care providers. There are so many organisations that can help. Most agencies specialise in particular conditions or areas. I will list a few of these organisations and their resources a little later.

Family members and close friends can also play a crucial role in your care journey, as their support may alleviate some of the burdens associated with transitioning from hospital to home. Your support network is very important. The lack of home care to support the patient's hospital-to-home transition is the number one cause of readmission of patients recently discharged from hospital. The first 72 hours after discharge from hospital stay is critical time for a patient. Discharged patients often still require acute care, assistance with washing, changing and changes in daily routine, like medications, diet regimens, rehab activities, physiotherapy and more. Poor or non-existent care during this critical period can lead to serious complications. If you don't have a support network, you have to try to create one. Engaging with community resources providers can provide not only practical assistance but also the emotional support, which is invaluable during a health crisis. This can be important if you don't have anyone close to you.

As you embark on creating your care plan and begin preparing for a Self-Directed assessment, remember to prioritise your mental well being alongside your physical health. After hospitalisation, recovery at home can bring its own set of challenges, and it's crucial to acknowledge and address mental health needs as part of the overall care strategy. Fresh air, movement and social activity can make a world of difference. With the right support and a well-structured care plan, you can navigate this transition successfully, ensuring that your return home is not just a change of address, but a step towards regaining independence and enhancing your quality of life.

Why Do Self-Directed Assessments Matter?

Health is a big issue: You may already know that your physical health is linked to your emotional health. How you feel affects your mental health, your financial health, your ability to work, and your ability take care of yourself. Your health affects your life outcomes. Your health also affects your enjoyment of food. It affects your dreams and the quality of your sleep. Your health basically affects every area of your life and every effort should be made to preserve and protect your health.

Care is a big business: This is why the people who need care are called 'Clients'. The care journey will most likely be challenging. The government in the UK spends inordinate amounts of money on domiciliary care, and only about a quarter (23%) is self funded. A 2024 report found that adult social care (including home care) contributed over £68.1 billion to the economy in England – up by 13.2% since 2022/23. Domiciliary care provider services in England increased by 63%, from 8,414 in 2017 to 13,733 in 2024. By contrast, nursing home occupancy decreased by 5% in the same period (and by 11% for those without nursing). The adult social care domiciliary care sector is bigger than the home rental and food services industry, but demand is outstripping supply and people are still finding it difficult to access appropriate care services

Care costs more if you delay: Yet, when it comes to healthcare services and support at home, most people are not investing in care planning, or getting the help when they actually need it. Instead, most people prefer to wait, until their situation becomes so out of control that they become too physically and or mentally unstable to make their own decisions and they are more vulnerable. It can also be very difficult to navigate the care system, as different local trusts have different care pathways and finding good options can be a lifeline. The best thing to do is to start planning your care routine early. Try to get it done before you reach the point where you are physically incapable of bending down to clean the skirting, or to confused get a cleaner in to help with housework, or have someone come in to cook nutritious meals for you. You can start with having someone come in and get 2-3 days worth of meals prepared and placed in Tupperware, to be refrigerated or frozen, then reheated, and eaten, instead of eating ready meals.

Another thing that most people, who have had their care assessment and care package arranged by a local authority or hospital discharge team fail to do, is speak up about the care tasks they actually need doing, and so those tasks are often inappropriately assessed. For example, Kate might have early onset dementia and a neck of femur fracture, and mobility issues. Kate might also suffer from minor incontinence, but not address the bladder weakness during her assessment, because Kate usually purchases discreet incontinence pads and feels she want to deal with this part of her care on her own. Addressing the issue of incontinence might feel upsetting and disorienting at first, but this problem can often be managed well with, supplements, continence care and good hygiene support. If left untreated the incontinence could become moderate to severe, and this may lead to a urinary tract infection. It's not just the elderly that may need extra support. More and more people are now getting debilitating, heart conditions, cancer and autoimmune conditions in there 30's and 40's. Have you thought about what support you would need, if you developed a physical or mental impairment, illness or disability?

When you lose control over your body, you can feel extremely fragile and vulnerable. This means your care assessment will matter. How well you are cared for, and the services you receive, decides your future. It's really that simple. Poor care leads to poor outcomes.

Self-Directed assessments play a crucial role in the care and support of patient's post-hospital discharge, especially for those navigating complex benefits like Personal Independence Payment (PIP) and Disability Living Allowance (DLA). A Self-Directed Care Assessments empowers care users and their families to take an active role in determining their individual care needs. By allowing service users to evaluate their specific circumstances, preferences, and goals, the Self-Directed assessment facilitates a tailored approach to home care that recognises the unique challenges you may face during the next step of recovery. The personalised Self-Directed approach not only enhances the quality of care received, but also promotes a sense of autonomy and dignity for people unhappy with their current care and patients transitioning from hospital to home.

One of the primary benefits of a Self-Directed assessment is that it helps to identify different and specific types of support required for a successful recovery. After a long and difficult stay in hospital, on discharge many patients run into various challenges, from mobility issues to difficulty managing daily tasks. By engaging in a Self-Directed assessment, you can pinpoint your needs, whether it's assistance with personal care, meal preparation, medication management, or companionship. This clarity enables families and caregivers to better seek out the most appropriate home care services, and ensure that every aspect of the care and recovery process is addressed effectively. Moreover, a Self-Directed assessment can help foster open communication between your family members, and home care providers. This collaboration can be a vital part in creating a care plan that reflects your individual preferences and lifestyle. Your family, or close friends should actively participate in the assessment process and help share insights about your habits and routines. Family involvement demonstrates that the service user is cared about and helps carers get to know their clients well enough to contribute towards their personalised care.

When home care workers understand the subtle moods and traits that make their clients unique, they are better equipped to offer the care and support that aligns with the client's daily life, ultimately leading to a smoother transition into care at home and a more comfortable ongoing or recovery experience.

In addition to facilitating personalised care, the Self-Directed assessment process also highlights the importance of interviewing potential home care workers. You can use the insights gained from the assessment process to interview and select caregivers who not only possess the necessary skills but also resonate with your personality and preferences. The interview process is essential for establishing a trusting relationship, which can significantly impact the quality of care received. By asking the right questions and taking the time to find the right match, your family can ensure that you feel supported and understood during your care.

Understanding the financial implications of home care is another critical aspect of Self-Directed assessments. Service users should explore different funding options, and entitlements, such as applying for financial assistance through Personal Independence Payments (PIP) or Disability Living Allowance (DLA), to help alleviate the financial burden associated with home care services. These benefits are not automatic. So by incorporating the budget considerations into the assessment process, you and your family can get clarity and make informed decisions about getting the level of care that align with your financial situation. This is a strategic approach that not only empowers you to access more of the care you need, but also promotes peace of mind during the transition into care.

A Self-Directed Assessment can help you to create a robust care plan that can not only address your immediate health needs but also works towards supporting your long-term well-being. Better care can lead to better outcomes, better outcomes could lead to better recovery, which substantially reduces or eliminates care costs.

Key Benefits of Self-Directed Assessments

Self-Directed assessments offer a range of key benefits for service users navigating the complexities of care. One of the primary advantages is the empowerment it provides to clients and their family following a hospital discharge. You are in charge and by taking an active role in determining your own care needs; you can ensure that your unique circumstances and preferences are taken into account. This personalised approach not only fosters a sense of control but also make sure that the care is appropriate and enhances client satisfaction with the care received, as the personalised care plan will align more closely with the your individual lifestyle and requirements.

Another significant benefit of having a Self-Directed assessment is the potential for improved communication between your family, and care providers. If you cannot speak for yourself, when someone speaks for you and properly articulates your needs and expectations, it sets the stage for clearer dialogues with home care agencies, care workers and support services. Families can become advocates for their loved ones, and more effectively communicate specific needs that may otherwise be overlooked. The collaborative effort can lead to a better care experience, where everyone involved is on the same page about the goals and methods of care that will work for you.

Self-Directed Assessments also enhance the efficiency of the care planning process. By identifying specific needs early on, you can streamline the process of finding suitable home care services. The proactive approach means less time spent searching for appropriate resources down the line, when things are going downhill. It means more time is spent on having exactly what you need and focusing on your recovery.

With the right information and tools, you can quickly locate specialised home care options tailored to the unique challenges faced by patients transitioning from hospital to home, and ensure a smoother adjustment period to the care.

Financial considerations are another critical aspect of the Self-Directed assessment. By accurately outlining your care needs early on and answering questions like: How many steps can you take without support? What medications you take? What stage your condition is at? You can better understand your potential eligibility for the various support programs available, and even complete their applications for benefits such as Personal Independence Payment and Disability Living Allowance, or the equivalent Universal Credit (UC) Component. Having clarity on your entitlement can make a significant difference in budgeting for care services, and it allows families to make informed financial decisions. Knowing what assistance is available can alleviate some of the stress associated with funding care, and enable your family to focus more on your well-being and less on the costs.

Lastly, Self-Directed Assessments can contribute to a stronger support network for those recovering at home. By engaging in the assessment process, families can identify not only the immediate care needs but also the resources that will support their loved ones mental health and overall well-being. The holistic approach recognises that recovery is not just a physical journey; it encompasses emotional and psychological aspects as well. A Self-Directed Assessment fosters a supportive environment and by seeking appropriate resources, families can significantly enhance the quality of life for their loved ones during the crucial post-hospital care, loss of capacity and palliative care decisions. Tools like Advance Statements and Lasting Power of Attorney (LPA) can make your support network even stronger.

What is an Advance Statement?
You may not need a care assessment right now, but if you're already thinking about your health and future, it may be a good idea for you to have a pre prepared Advance Statement of your care wishes. An Advance Statement is a personal record of your wishes, feelings, beliefs, and values. Writing an Advance Statement is a valuable first step. It can help to guide others if you become unwell and need care or medical treatment.

Understanding Your Advance Statement
The main purpose of an Advance Statement is to

ensure that if you ever lose the ability to make or communicate decisions, that those around you—whether family, carers, or healthcare professionals—will have a clear understanding of what matters most to you. While an Advance Statement is not legally binding, every healthcare professional must take it into account when making decisions on your behalf.

To keep your Advance Statement easily accessible, scan and email a copy to yourself, store it with important documents like your photo ID and banking information, and consider sharing it with your GP so it can be added to your medical records.

What to Include in Your Advance Statement

An Advance Statement can cover any aspect of your future health or social care. It helps you think through and record the things that are most important to you. You don't need to fill in every section—just the ones that matter to you.

Here are some key areas to consider:
Preferences & Boundaries

What aspects of care do you prefer not to experience?
Would you prefer not to be taken to hospital?
Is receiving personal care from a member of the opposite sex unacceptable to you?

Your Health & Communication Needs

What signs indicate that you're feeling unwell?

How do you best communicate your feelings and needs

to others?

Do you have any concerns, such as managing pain or avoiding sedation?

Your Daily Life & Activities

What activities bring you joy—spending time with loved ones, listening to music, reading?

Where do you enjoy doing these activities, how often, and with whom?

Consider including outdoor activities to reflect on your lifestyle and preferences.

Your Identity & Personal Expression

What aspects of your life are fundamental to your identity?

What name do you prefer to be called?

How do you like to dress?

How do you care for, and style your hair?

How important are independence, privacy, and dignity to you?

What are your religious or spiritual beliefs?

Your Care Preferences & Routine

Do you have a daily routine you'd like to maintain?

What time do you wake up or go to bed?

Do you prefer a bath or a shower?

What can you manage independently, and where might you need assistance?

By taking the time to write your Advance Statement, while you have the mental capacity, you create a road map for your future care that respects your wishes, values, and identity.

How to Create an Advance Statement

You can create your own Advance Statement in a PDF, Word, or Text document to outline your personal preferences and important considerations for your care.

Step 1: Title Your Document

At the top of your document, write: Advance Statement

Step 2: Provide Your Personal Details Include the following information:

Name
Date of birth Address
Email address Phone number
GP details (GP's name, phone number, and address)

Step 3: Define Your Preferences

Create sections for each of the following topics and number and begin each paragraph with the suggested prompt:

The things that are important in my life are…
The things that are important to my identity are… My religious or spiritual beliefs are…
The things I do not like are…
Important information to know when caring for me…
My food needs and preferences are…
The place I would like to be cared for is…
The Important people in my life are…

Step 4: Identify Your Care Decision Supporters
Include this statement: "I have discussed this Advance Statement with the following people and would like them to be involved in decisions about my care."
List their details:
Name Relationship Phone number

Step 5: Finalise Your Statement:
At the bottom of the document, sign and date your Advance Statement to make it official.

Understanding Lasting Power of Attorney
Putting someone in charge of your care is another option. There are two type of Lasting Power of Attorney (LPA) that give people close to you the power to act for you if you lose capacity. One LPA is for Financial and Property and the other is for Health and Welfare.

Creating a Lasting Power of Attorney (LPA) for Health and Welfare helps to ensure that your personal choices regarding medical treatment, daily care, and living arrangements are respected, even if you lose the ability to make decisions for yourself. By appointing someone close to you to act as your attorney, you grant him or her legal authority to enforce your wishes—whether it's refusing certain treatments, choosing where you receive care, or safeguarding your dignity in critical situations. This legal safeguard becomes especially crucial in cases where complex decisions, such as life-sustaining treatment or potential deprivation of liberty under the Mental Capacity Act. An attorney can advocate on your behalf, challenge inappropriate restrictions, and ensure your rights are upheld, giving you peace of mind that your future care aligns with your values.

Finding Lasting Power of Attorney

If you want to be super organised in your care planning and take things up notch Here's a step-by-step guide to applying for a Lasting Power of Attorney (LPA) for Health and Welfare in the UK:

Step 1: Download the Application Form: You can download the LPA for Health and Welfare (LP1H) form from the UK government website. Alternatively, you can complete the application online.

Step 2: Choose Your Attorney(s): Select one or more trusted individuals to act as your attorney(s). They must be over 18 and capable of making decisions on your behalf.

Step 3: Find a Certificate Provider: A certificate provider is the person who confirms that you understand the LPA and are not being pressured into making it. They must be: A professional (e.g., a doctor, solicitor, or social worker), OR a friend or associate (not a relatives), Someone who has known you personally for at least two years.

Step 4: Get the Document Witnessed: Someone over the age of 18 must be witness to your signature. Attorneys must also sign the document, and their signatures must be witnessed.

Step 5: Notify Relevant People (Optional): You can notify up to five people about your LPA before registration. This adds an extra layer of security, allowing them to raise concerns if necessary.

Step 6: Submit the Application: Send the completed form to the Office of the Public Guardian (OPG) at the address provided on the form.

Step 7: Pay the Registration Fee: The standard fee for registering a LPA is currently £82. If you receive certain benefits or have a low income, you may qualify for a fee reduction or exemption.

Step 8: Wait for Registration: The OPG will review your application, which typically takes up to 10 weeks. If there are no objections, your LPA will be registered and become legally valid.

Step 9: Handling Objections: If someone objects to your LPA, the OPG will investigate. Objections can be raised on grounds such as: The donor lacked mental capacity when making the LPA. The attorney is unsuitable or acting improperly. The LPA was made under undue pressure. If an objection is raised, the matter may be referred to the Court of Protection, which will decide whether the LPA should proceed.

Life and relationships can be complex. If you have relatives who are likely to challenge your choice of attorney, you may want to consider making an Advance Statement instead. Navigating an objection to a Lasting Power of Attorney (LPA) for Health and Welfare in the Court of Protection can be complex, and the likelihood of success depends on the nature of the objection and the strength of the evidence presented.

Pro Se (Self-Representation) vs. Professional Legal Representation Pro Se Representation:

While it is possible to represent yourself, the Court of Protection deals with intricate legal and medical matters and objections often require detailed arguments backed by expert opinions. Success in self-representation depends on your ability to present clear, well-supported evidence.

Professional Legal Representation:

Hiring a solicitor or barrister significantly improves your chances, especially if the objection involves claims of undue influence, fraud, or lack of mental capacity. Costs vary, but legal fees can range from £2,000 to £10,000, depending on complexity and whether a hearing is required.

Costs Involved:
Court Application Fee: £421.

Legal Fees: Solicitor fees vary widely, but complex cases requiring hearings can exceed £10,000.

Expert Reports: If medical or capacity assessments are needed, additional costs may apply.

Difficulty and Duration Straightforward Cases:
If the objection is weak or lacks evidence, the process may be resolved within a few months.

Complex Cases:
If hearings are required, the process can take six months to over a year.

Urgent Cases: The Court of Protection can fast-track urgent matters, but this is rare. If you were to make an application for LPA and faced objections, help, information and guidance on preparing evidence or responding to objections effectively can be found at the following links.

https://www.gov.uk/object-registration-power-attorney

https://ukcareguide.co.uk/court-of-protection/

Useful links for planning ahead:
Age UK: Advance decisions, advance statements and living wills (PDF: 436kb) (Link:

https://www.ageuk.org.uk/globalassets/ageuk/documents/factsheets/fs72_advance_decisions_advance_statements_and_living_wills_fcs.pdf)

Alzheimer's Society: Advance statements and dementia (Link: https://www.alzheimers.org.uk/getsupport/legal-financial/what-is-advance- statement)

Cancer Research UK: Advance care planning (Link: http://www.cancerresearchuk.org/aboutcancer/coping/dying-with-cancer/making- plans/care-planning)

Compassion in Dying: How we can help (Link: https://compassionindying.org.uk/how-we-canhelp/)

Planning ahead for end of life care (Link: www.nhs.uk/conditions/end-of-lifecare/planning-ahead/)

Why plan ahead for end of life care? (Link: https://www.nhs.uk/conditions/end-of-lifecare/planning-ahead/why-plan-ahead/)

Advance decision to refuse treatment (living will) (Link: https://www.nhs.uk/conditions/end-of-lifecare/planning-ahead/advance-decision- to-refuse-treatment/)

Lasting power of attorney (Link: https://www.nhs.uk/conditions/end-of-life-care/planningahead/lasting-power-of-attorney/)

Chapter 2: Navigating the Self-Directed Assessment Process

In this chapter, we'll explore how people can request a Self-Directed Assessment from their local council, whether they are receiving benefits or not. We will also discuss how pensioners can access support and how to apply for NHS Continuing Healthcare.

Requesting a Self-Directed assessment is an important step for anyone seeking personalised care options after a progressive health or disability worsens, or a hospital discharge. To initiate this process, you first need to identify the appropriate agency or local authority that manages assessments in your area. This could be your local council or an independent organisation specialising in care assessments. If you have a social worker this is your first point of call. Send them an email and tell them you want to know the procedure for a Self- Directed Care Assessment and that you require an urgent response. Visit their website or contact them directly to inquire about their specific procedures.

Gathering your personal information, medical history, and any relevant documentation ahead of time will help to streamline the process and ensure that your needs are clearly articulated. When you make your request, be clear about your circumstances and the reasons for needing a Self-Directed assessment. Explain your recent hospital discharge and any ongoing health issues or mobility challenges you may be facing. It's beneficial to highlight how these factors influence your daily living and the type of support you require. Your honesty and clarity will help the assessment team understand your unique situation, allowing them to tailor their services to fit your needs.

After your request has been submitted, you will typically be contacted for an initial conversation or meeting. This is your opportunity to discuss your situation in detail and express any specific preferences you have regarding your care.

Make sure to ask questions about the assessment process, what support options are available, and how care plans are developed. This dialogue can empower you to take an active role in shaping your care, ensuring that the services you receive align with your personal goals and lifestyle.

Once the assessment process is completed, you will receive a care plan outlining the recommended services and support. Take the time to review this document thoroughly and ensure that it reflects your needs. If you feel that certain aspects are missing or need adjustment, don't hesitate to reach out to the assessment team for clarification or modifications. Remember, this plan is meant to work for you and enhance your quality of life, so advocating for yourself is crucial.

As you navigate the search for suitable home care and support workers, utilise local resources, community groups, and online platforms to find qualified professionals. Consider interviewing potential caregivers to ensure they not only have the necessary skills but also align with your personal preferences and values. This careful selection process will help you build a supportive environment that fosters your recovery and well being at home.

How to Request a Self-Directed Assessment If You Are Receiving PIP, New Style ESA, DLA, or Other Disability Benefits

Requesting a Self-Directed assessment can be an essential step for those receiving benefits such as Personal Independence Payment (PIP), New Style Employment and Support Allowance (ESA), Disability Living Allowance (DLA), or other disability benefits. This process allows you to tailor your care and support according to your unique needs, especially if you've recently been discharged from the hospital.

To initiate this request, the first step is to contact your local authority or the relevant agency managing your benefits. They will provide guidance on the specific forms and information required to start the assessment process.

If you are receiving benefits such as Personal Independence Payment (PIP), New Style Employment and Support Allowance (ESA), Daily Living Component of PIP, Armed Forces Independence Payment, Constant Attendance Allowance, or the Disability Living Allowance (DLA) component of Universal Credit, you may be eligible for a Self-Directed Assessment.

Step-by-Step Process:

1. Contact Your Local Council: The first step is to contact your local council's social services or adult care services department. You can usually find their contact details on the council's website or by calling their general inquiries number.

2. Explain Your Current Benefits and Needs: Let the council know that you are receiving one of the eligible benefits and explain your needs. You might be asked for some details about how your condition affects your daily life and why you need care or support.

3. Request a Self-Directed Assessment: You MUST specifically ask for a Self-Directed Assessment. Do not agree to a Direct, or Directed Care Assessment. Self-Directed means you want to be involved in planning your care, choosing your carers, and managing payments if necessary. The council will likely provide you with forms to complete or schedule an assessment with a care worker.

4. Provide Documentation of Your Benefits: Be prepared to provide documents related to your benefits to support your request. This could include your PIP award letter or proof of your other benefit claims.

5. Agree on a Care Plan and Funding Options: After the assessment, you will be able to choose how you receive support and whether you want to use Direct Payments. The council will help you create a care plan, and if you qualify, they may set up Direct Payments or arrange a Direct Payment Card for you to manage the cost of care.

6. Review and Finalise Your Care Plan: After the assessment, you will have the opportunity to review the proposed care plan and discuss any changes before it is finalised.

When you reach out for a Self-Directed assessment, be prepared to discuss your individual circumstances, including your health condition, daily challenges, and the type of support you believe would benefit you most. Keep a daily dairy for a week or two before your assessment. Write down how often you use the bathroom, how often you wash, and or comb your hair, what task you have trouble with, when you eat, what type of meals you eat and how long they take to prepare, how often you drink, pain, allergies, medical conditions, prescriptions taken, what type of exercise you need, what type of social activities you enjoy. Describe in detail the support you will need. This conversation is crucial; as it helps the professionals understand your specific needs and preferences, allowing them to create a care plan that truly reflects your situation. Getting it done may be a struggle, but it's worth it.

Additionally, keep any relevant medical or support documents handy, as these can provide valuable context to the assessors regarding your daily living requirements.

Once your request is submitted, you will typically be scheduled for an assessment meeting. During this meeting, it is important to communicate openly about your experiences and the support you require. Be honest about your limitations and aspirations, as this will help ensure that the assessment accurately captures your needs. You might also want to involve family members or caregivers in this meeting, as they can provide additional insights and support your case for receiving the necessary care.

After the assessment, you will receive a report detailing the recommendations for your care. Take the time to review this document carefully and ensure it aligns with your expectations. If you find that certain needs have not been adequately addressed or if you disagree with the recommendations, you have the right to appeal the decision or request a reassessment. It's essential to advocate for yourself and ensure that your care plan meets your needs.

Finally, once your Self-Directed assessment is approved, you can begin exploring home care options that suit your requirements. This includes researching and interviewing potential care workers who can provide the necessary support.

Remember, finding the right caregiver is crucial to your recovery or ongoing care needs and well-being. Consider creating a list of questions to ask during interviews, focus on the carer's experience, qualifications, and compatibility with your personal preferences. With the right support in place, you can transition smoothly from hospital to home, ensuring a comfortable and safe recovery environment.

Paying for Care
Home Care is expensive (the NHS estimates an

average £400 to £800 a week). If you have to move into a care home the average weekly residential care home cost is £1,402, and £1,597 a week, for intensive nursing and dementia care. One in eight people will need extensive care that exceeds the above costs.

Those who believe they can afford to pay the full costs of their care may not want to undergo a full financial assessment. They may just want their local council to arrange the care and support, and they can ask the local authority the carry out a 'light-touch' financial assessment, if they do not want to undergo the detailed process. If the local authority is satisfied that the person will continue to be able to afford the cost of their care for the distant future, they may agree to this.

After the financial assessment, the local authority will tell you whether you need to pay for all or some of your care costs.

How Does The Local Authority Charge For Care and Support?
First, your local authority will assess the applicant and decide whether they have eligible care needs. The local authority will then work with the person to consider what types of support might be provided to meet their needs. However, unlike NHS healthcare, local authority commissioned care and support is not free to use. Everyone has to contribute something towards their care costs, and care costs of £25,000+ per annum are not unusual and will absorb most average incomes. The local authority may pay a contribution towards

care costs. Currently, only people with savings and assets of less than £23,250 and those on low incomes receive any help from the local authority with their care and support costs. People who develop long-term or severe care and support needs will usually face substantial costs before they can eventually get financial support from the government. In cases where the costs of care are so high, that you would not be able to live from day to day after paying for your care costs. Then the local authority will pay some of the care costs to make sure that you are left with this minimum level of income. This approach ensures people will still receive the care they need, even when they have a modest income that could pay all the care costs, but not leave them enough to live on.

Anyone can ask their local authority, regardless of their finances, to arrange their care and support for them. This is a safeguard that makes it less likely for people who are uncertain about the care system, or their entitlement to care, to not arrange their care plans and to go without help and support. However, they will still need to pay for their care and support if they have adequate financial resources.

The Care Act was supposed to put a total £86,000 cap on people's lifetime liabilities for their personal care costs, based on how much the person's council would – or does – pay for meeting the individual's care needs, except where the person is receiving means-tested support, in which case only their individual contributions (not the money they receive from other benefits) count towards the cap. The care cap was scheduled for 2023, the plan being, once the individual had reached the cap on payment of care costs their local authority could not charge them anything further towards the costs of meeting their care and support needs. However this proposed cap was scrapped.

"Right now, councils are being pushed to the brink with rising adult social care costs, children's placements and temporary accommodation," said Pete Marland, the chair of the LGA's economy and resources board.

To decide what a person can afford to pay, a local authority will carry out a financial assessment. The local authority will consider the person's income and any assets they own, like a house or other investments. The local authority will then calculate how much the person can afford to pay towards their care and support costs.

If people are due to pay charges for their care and support, they may be entitled to a 'deferred payment agreement', through which they delay charges, and repay the local authority at a later date.

Your home may also be considered an asset. Sometimes a homeowner may want to consider a 'deferred payment agreement' with the local authority. This is an arrangement whereby the person agrees, with their local authority, to pay some of their fees at a later date. This means they should not be forced to sell their home during their lifetime, to pay for their care. The person usually repays the local authority from the sale of their property or it is repaid from their estate.

Your Capital/Savings and What You Will Have to Pay

If you live in England have over £23,250 in Savings and Assets. You have to pay your own fees as a 'self-funder'.

Capital limits

Capital limits are the savings or assets (excluding any capital that has been disregarded) that a person can have while qualifying for financial support from their local authority.

For England the financial year (2025 to 2026), if you have between £14,250 and £23,250 you qualify for financial support from the council and pay a contribution from your income – such as pensions – plus a 'tariff income' based on your capital. This 'tariff income' is worked out by assuming you have an extra £1 per week in income for every £250 (or part of) you have between £14,250 and £23,250 in capital.

If you have Less than £14,250 the council provides financial support and you will still have to contribute from your income, but you won't have to pay a tariff income.

The Capital limits are different for **England, Scotland, Northern Ireland and Wales.** The upper capital limits and Lower capital limits are England £23,250 - £14,250; Scotland £35,000 - £21,500; Wales £50,000 – n/a; Northern Ireland £23,250 -£14,250. Mostly, the Capital Limits are pretty similar, except for Wales, where you are not required to contribute from you savings, unless you have over £50,000 in assets.

So for instance, a person living in England with savings or assets above £23,250 (the upper capital limit) is responsible for the full cost of their care cost or their care home costs, until their saving and assets fall below £23,250.

A person with assets between the £14,250 - £23,250 capital limits will pay what they can afford from their income, plus £1 per week for every £250 of capital over £14.250. This is called a means-tested contribution from assets.

So for example, if you had £15.250 in savings, you would pay £4 a week extra towards your care costs. If you had £17.250 in savings, you would pay £12 a week extra towards your care costs.

A person with savings and assets below £14.250 (the lower capital limit) will only pay their care costs, from what they can afford from their income.

Personal Expenses Allowance
If you live in a care home, because the home is supposed to provide all food, shelter and utilities, only a very small amount of you income will be exempt

from paying for your care. A Personal Expenses Allowance (PEA) is the weekly amount that people receiving local authority-arranged care and support in a care home (residents) are assumed to need as a minimum for their personal expenses. For the financial year (2025 to 2026), the PEA is £30.65 per week.

The Minimum Income Guarantee
A person receiving local authority-arranged care and support in their own home need to have a certain amount of income to cover their living costs. Under the Care Act 2014, care cost must not reduce people's income below a certain amount. This is a weekly amount that you can keep and not have to spend on care costs; this money could come from Universal credit, pensions, employment or investments. This is known as the Minimum Income Guarantee MIG, applicable for the financial year (2025 to 2026).

If you are a single person: —
Aged 18 or older but less than 25, the amount of your income you get to keep is £89.15 per week.

If you are aged 25 or older but less than pension credit age, the amount of your income you get to keep is £112.50 per week.

If you have reached pension credit age (67), the amount of your income you get to keep is £232.60 per week.

If you are a lone parent aged 18 or over:

The amount of your income you get to keep is £112.50 per week. Plus if you are responsible for children, who live in your household, the additional amount of your income you get to keep is £102.95 per child

If you live with your spouse or partner—
If you are both aged 18 or over, the amount is £88.35 per week.

If one or both of you have attained pension credit age, the amount of your income you get to keep is £177.55 per week.

Disability benefits are financial support payments that help you if you have a very low income or no income and can't work, or work reduced hours, because of sickness or disability. The council can apply the money you receive from income benefits like ESA, PIP towards your care costs.

If you are single person who is in receipt of disability benefit, or the local authority considers that you should, be in receipt of income support, or a disability premium, the income from the benefit entitlement is used towards your care costs. The amount of the benefit you don't have to pay out towards paying for your care cost and are allowed to keep is considered a premium. The amount of the premium for a general disability benefit is £49.65 per week.

If you receive an enhanced disability benefit, the amount of the applicable premium is £24.25 per week.

If you live with your partner and one member of the couple is in receipt of a disability premium, the amount of the applicable premium you can keep is £35.40 per week.

If you live with your partner and you receive an enhanced disability benefit, the amount of the applicable premium is £17.45 per week.

If you are receiving Carer benefits, the amount of the applicable premium is £53.25 per week.

Savings Credit
A second part to pension credit is called savings credit which is only available for those who reached state pension age before 6 April 2016, and who have some form of retirement savings, for example in a workplace or personal pension.

Savers who put money into their retirement funds during their working life and don't qualify for a pension credit top-up, but who could do with a little extra money on top of what they've already put aside might still be eligible for savings credit. Single eligible people get up to £17.30 savings credit a week, while couples can get £19.36.

After totalling up your income and savings, if you think you could still be eligible for savings credit, then it is definitely worth applying. Even if you are only eligible for a very small top-up, it entitles you to other benefits that could be worth much more in total. For example, you automatically receive cold weather payments, and can get help with NHS costs such as dental treatment.

Every little help and income you get from Savings Credit that doesn't have to be applied to your care costs. The amount of savings credit you can receive will depend on how much income you get. To work it out your savings credit entitlement you need to add up your total income.

For example, add together your state pension income, private pension income and your savings income to get your total weekly income. To work out your savings income under the government rules, every £500 you have above a £10,000 threshold equates to £1 of weekly income. Let's say you have £16,500 in savings. To work out the savings income, you would take your £16,500 and deduct £10,000. You then divide the remaining £6,500 by £500 that would add up to £13 weekly income.

For every £1 in income over the pension credit thresholds of £198.27 a week for single people and £314.34 for couples your credit entitlement would be reduced by 40p.

How To Claim Pension Savings Credit?
You can apply online for pension savings credit at Gov.uk or you can call the Pension Credit Claim Line

on 0800 99 1234 (text phone 0800 169 0133).

Some types of income, such as certain disability benefits, are not included in the means test. The same applies to specific forms of capital. However, all other income and assets may be considered.
If the means test shows you're eligible for help with care costs, you might still need to contribute toward the cost. When calculating this amount, the council must ensure your income doesn't drop below a minimum level, known as the minimum income guarantee. This is currently £232.60 per week if you're single and over State Pension age, or £175.55 per week if you're part of a couple where one or both partners are over State Pension age.

If you qualify for help with home care costs, you can either have the council arrange the care services for you or receive a direct payment—money paid directly to you— so you can organise your own care.

How to Request a Self-Directed Assessment Without Claiming Benefits

Even if you are not receiving any of the qualifying benefits mentioned above, you could still request a Self-Directed Assessment through your local council even if you are privately funding your care. This could apply to people who have a disability or care need but do not claim government benefits.

1. Contact Your Local Council: Reach out to your

local council's adult social care services. They may have a contact form on their website or a direct phone number for care-related inquiries.

2. Assess Your Needs: You will need to explain why you need help with daily tasks, health issues, or mobility. You may be asked to provide information on your condition and how it impacts your day-to-day life.

3. Request a Self-Directed Assessment: If your needs are assessed and considered eligible, you can request to have a Self-Directed Assessment. Do not agree to a Direct, or Directed Assessment or any other type of assessment. Self-Directed means you want to be involved in planning your care. This allows you to take control of your care plan, including deciding on your carers and how your support is arranged.

4. Be Prepared for an Assessment: You might be required to undergo an initial assessment by a social worker or care coordinator. Draft a care plan with a schedule of tasks to help the assessor evaluate your needs and discuss your preferences.

5. Review the Options for Funding: If your assessment is approved, the council will discuss potential options for funding, including Direct Payments or a Direct Payment Card, so you can manage your own care.

6. Create Your Care Plan: Once the assessment is completed, you will work with your local council to create a care plan tailored to your needs.

If you have over £23,250 in savings, you have to pay your own fees as a 'self-funder'. Requesting a self-directed assessment without claiming benefits can feel daunting, but it is an empowering step toward gaining control over your care plan. The first step in this process is to contact your local authority or relevant care provider. You may not be in receipt of benefits, but you still have the right to request an assessment based on your individual needs. If you have been hospitalised and are being discharged, NHS Continuing Care is not means tested. You could receive a care package funded by the NHS for a period of time. Explain your situation clearly, emphasising that you are seeking support for your care requirements post-hospital discharge.

Once you have made contact, it's beneficial to prepare for the assessment. It is essential to be ready to communicate ALL your specific needs and how they may be influenced by your recent hospitalisation, as this context will help the assessor understand the urgency and importance of your request. Gather any relevant documentation that outlines your medical history, current health status, and any support you may already have. This information can provide the assessor with a clearer picture of your situation. Additionally, prepare a schedule of care tasks, with your goals and preferences for care. This could include the specific types of support you feel would be most beneficial, such as assistance with daily living activities or companionship. Being well prepared and having a plan, will not only streamline the assessment process, but will also demonstrate that you have a proactive approach to managing your care.

During the assessment, be open and honest about your needs. The assessor will ask questions that may cover various aspects of your life, including physical health, mental well being, and social connections. It is crucial to articulate how your hospital discharge has impacted your daily routines and what kind of help you envision would make your transition back home smoother. Create a care plan in advance. This is your opportunity to advocate for yourself and ensure that your care plan reflects your unique circumstances and preferences.

If you can create a care plan, with the Care Plan Assistant app, learn more @ www.CareCoaching.co.uk After the assessment, you will receive a local authority care plan outlining the support that can be arranged. If the plan meets your needs, you can move forward with implementing it. If not, do not hesitate to express any concerns, draft your own plan, or make requests for adjustments. Remember, it is essential that you are comfortable and satisfied with the care you receive. You have the right to advocate for changes and seek clarification on any aspects of the plan that may not align with your expectations or needs.

Finding a good home care support worker is a crucial element of your care plan. Don't just rely on Council Commissioned Care Services. Check out all the resources available to you, such as local support groups or online care agencies to identify potential candidates. If you're paying for your own care (known as self-funding), you can choose and arrange care services yourself. However, if you have eligible care needs and would rather the local council handle this on your behalf, they are required to do so—though they may charge an arrangement fee.

The cost of home care is typically around £20 -£25 per hour, but this can vary based on factors such as your location and the level of support you need. It's a good idea to contact several home care providers in your area to compare services and prices, helping you find the option that best suits your needs. Some online agencies allow you to choose you carers and you can interview them by video call.

When interviewing a new home care worker, ask them about their experience, training, and approach to care. Trust your instincts; the right support worker should make you feel comfortable and respected. By taking these steps, you can create a supportive environment that facilitates your recovery and enhances your quality of life, ensuring that your transition from hospital to home is as seamless as possible.

If you feel you, or someone caring for you may be entitled to benefits please check out the links below https://www.gov.uk/carers-allowance/eligibility

If you only get basic support, your carer could get

£83.30 a week if they care for you at least 35 hours a week and they get certain benefits. They do not have to be related to you, or live with you

https://www.gov.uk/pip

Personal Independence Payment (PIP) replaces Disability Living Allowance (DLA) - to find out how and when to claim, rates, and eligibility.

https://www.gov.uk/attendance-allowance/eligibility

Attendance Allowance helps pay for your personal care if you've reached State Pension age and are disabled.

How Pensioners Can Request a Self-Directed Assessment

Pensioners seeking a self-directed assessment can take proactive steps to ensure they receive the care and support they need after being discharged from the hospital. The process begins with understanding your rights and the available options to tailor your care plan according to your specific needs.

It is essential to gather all relevant documentation, such as medical records and details about current benefits, which will help present, a comprehensive case for your assessment. This preparation will empower you in discussions with care providers and local authorities.

Pensioners who don't have severe dementia, or issue around mental capacity usually find that a Self

Directed Assessment is ideal for managing their care needs. In fact, pensioners often find the flexibility of a Self Directed Assessment is ideal for ensuring that they receive the best possible care, in a way that suits them.

Step-by-Step Process for Pensioners:
1. Contact the Local Council's Social Care Services: As with other groups, pensioners or their advocate should start by contacting the adult social care services in their area. This is usually done via the local council's website or by calling their contact centre.

2. Explain Care Needs and Circumstances: You will need to explain your care needs. For pensioners, these needs might include assistance with mobility, washing, dressing, or managing medication. If you have a medical condition or disability, be sure to mention it.

3. Request a Self-Directed Assessment: Once your needs are explained, you can specifically request a Self-Directed Assessment. This enables you to choose your carers, manage your care, and explore payment options like Direct Payments.

4. Assess Your Financial Situation (if applicable): While pensioners are typically eligible for support, especially if in receipt of Pension Credit. Some may also have to go through a financial assessment to determine how much funding they can receive from the local council. This is often based on income and savings.

5. Create Your Personalised Care Plan: After the assessment, the council will work with you and your advocate/s to create a care plan that meets your needs and preferences. This plan can include options for Direct Payments to allow you to control your care funding.

To initiate a Self-Directed assessment, pensioners should first contact their local council or the relevant agency responsible for adult social care. When reaching out, be clear about your situation and express your intent to request an assessment. It can be beneficial to have a trusted family member or friend accompany you during this process. They can help articulate your needs and support you in navigating any complexities that may arise. Remember, you are not alone; many resources are available to assist you in this journey.

Once your request is submitted, you may be invited for an assessment meeting where a social worker or care assessor will evaluate your situation. During this meeting, communicate openly about your daily challenges and what support you envision. It is an opportunity to discuss your preferences for home care and the types of assistance that would benefit you most. Be sure to ask questions about the assessment process and how decisions regarding your care will be made, as this will help you feel more informed and involved.

After the assessment, you will receive a personalised

care plan outlining the support services you are eligible for. This plan should reflect your individual needs and preferences, making it easier to find suitable home care options. If you feel that the recommendations do not align with your requirements, do not hesitate to voice your concerns. You have the right to appeal any decisions and seek adjustments that better suit your situation.

Finding a good home care and support worker is crucial for a smooth transition from hospital to home. Utilise the resources available to you, such as local directories, recommendations from healthcare professionals, and online platforms that specialise in home care services.

Take the time to interview potential caregivers to ensure they align with your values and understand your needs. With thorough preparation and a clear understanding of the Self-Directed assessment process, pensioners can confidently navigate their care options and enhance their quality of life at home.

Preparing for Your Assessment - Checklist and Notes

Preparing for your assessment is a critical step in ensuring that you receive the care and support you need. Using a checklist can make this process smoother and less overwhelming. Start by compiling all necessary documents, including medical records, previous assessments, and any supporting letters from healthcare professionals. This information will provide a comprehensive view of your needs and circumstances. Additionally, consider creating a personal statement that outlines your daily challenges and how they impact your life. This document can be a powerful tool during your assessment, showcasing the areas where you require assistance.

Next, take the time to evaluate your specific needs. Reflect on daily activities that pose challenges, such as personal care, mobility, and household tasks. Make a list of these difficulties, prioritising the tasks based on urgency and impact. This reflective process will not only help you articulate your needs during the assessment but also guide you in identifying the right type of support. Don't hesitate to involve family members or caregivers in this discussion, as they can provide valuable insights into your situation.

Moreover, you should familiarise yourself with the assessment process itself. Research what to expect during the assessment, including the types of questions that may be asked. Understanding the criteria used to evaluate your needs will help you prepare more effectively. Consider reaching out to local advocacy groups or organisations that specialise in helping care users navigate these assessments. They can provide additional resources and support, ensuring that you feel confident and well prepared on the day of your assessment.

When it comes to finding a suitable home care worker, take a proactive approach. Begin by identifying the qualities and skills you would like in a caregiver.

Create a list of questions to ask during interviews, focusing on their experience, training, and approach to care. This preparation can help you find someone who not only meets your practical needs but also aligns with your personal preferences. Remember, this is about creating a supportive environment where you feel comfortable and respected.

Lastly, keep in mind that financial considerations are an essential part of your planning. Research potential funding options to understand what assistance you may be eligible for. This knowledge can alleviate some of the stress associated with budgeting for care services. Make a note of any financial documents you may need to present and keep track of your expenditures related to care. By preparing thoroughly, you can approach your assessment with confidence, knowing you have taken the necessary steps to advocate for your needs and secure the appropriate support.

Common Challenges and How to Overcome Them

Most people accept council commissioned care, because the council is usually willing to pay its own agencies up to £25 per hour, for clients, but the agency will only give a client about £19.00- £21.00 in Direct payments per hour to pay for self chosen agency care and usually pay 1-2 weeks in arrears. People who are funding their own care should definitely find a good carer from an agency of their own choice. People who only receive Direct Payments are not really going to be able to afford good personal care without a council commissioned agency. Council commissioned agency carers often have multiple calls in the same location and can undertake half hour calls and double up carers.

Some care clients may need to allow the council to handle some of the personal care and lifting and handling and hire a private carer for other care needs, For example if you are not funding your own care, you may opt for council commissioned carers to handle your washing and changing. A private agency carer or PA can handle your laundry, hair care, cooking, shopping, housework, physiotherapy, or taking you out on outings?

Most people think their options are either Council Commissioned Care, or the provision of a Direct Payment card, which usually cannot used to pay family members, but generally not funded enough to pay for private care needed. Most people are not aware of the self-directed option. According to the In-Control booklet, "some councils talk about supported self-assessment as part of the process, but each local authority does things a bit differently." Some local authorities won't tell you about Self-Directed Support Assessments at all. Most people haven't heard of Self-Directed Care Support Assessments, and the residents of the disadvantaged boroughs, especially those with predominantly ethnic populations will almost certainly have to request the service. A care package is basically a list of services that a person will receive and a number of hours they will be allocated for each task. Someone from the council comes round and looks at your home and your health condition and then decides how much care you should receive and who is going to pay for it. That is generally how the care needs assessment process works.

Generally, it is not the best idea to put council social services in charge of the decision of what you need. The council generally has budgetary constraints that they will prioritise. The tendency not to disclose that there is an option for clients to decide what kind of care they need, is how councils stay in control of care assessment and the care package costs and they more often fund preferred agencies and services that might suit local authority requirements, but not fully meet the client's or service user's needs.

You must specifically request a "Self-Directed Care Assessment" for a funded care package and its best to do if in writing. If you contact the local authority adult social services and ask over the phone they will normally direct you to a team of staff and you will likely end up with a normal assessment. You can contact adult social services by email with a detailed request, before contacting the service by phone. All local authorities have websites and if you cannot get the email of the manager of adult social services go to your local library and they should be able to help you get the correct name and contact details.

If you think you might be interested in Self-Directed care and support assessment. The In Control service can give you advice on how you can fill out as much of care assessment on you own as you can, or with your family's help.

In Control can also provide you with help, if you have difficulty understanding information, or think you are going to have difficulty communicating your views to the person doing the assessment, and they can arrange an independent person, an advocate, to help you in the assessment. This independent advocate will understand how the local authority reaches decisions and will spend time with you to help you understand and be fully involved in the assessment, planning and review processes. In Control can also help you think about your needs and reach decisions about how you want them to be met. The person will help make sure you understand your rights and what you can expect from the local authority. The advocate can also help you challenge a decision made by the local authority. You can ask for an independent advocate at any point in the Self-Directed support assessment process.

For more information check out the **In Control** website at: www.in-control.org.uk

Navigating the complexities of Self-Directed assessments and home care can be daunting, especially during a transition from hospital to home. One common challenge people face is navigating the process of requesting a Self-Directed assessment.

Many feel overwhelmed by the paperwork and eligibility criteria, leading to delays or even avoidance.

To overcome this, it's essential to break down the process into manageable steps. Start by researching the specific requirements for your benefits, such as Personal Independence Payment (PIP) or Disability Living Allowance (DLA). Utilise resources provided by local authorities or disability advocacy groups, as they can offer guidance and support in filling out necessary forms and understanding your rights.

Another significant hurdle is finding the right home care and support worker tailored to your needs. Many people struggle with knowing what qualities to look for or how to evaluate potential candidates. To address this, create a clear list of your specific needs and preferences, including the skills, personality traits and experience that you think are important for your care.

Consider conducting interviews with potential caregivers to assess their compatibility and expertise. Don't hesitate to ask for references or check reviews from other clients. This proactive approach not only helps in finding the right fit, but also empowers you throughout the selection process.

Cost can be an additional barrier when seeking home cares services, especially for those on a budget. Understanding financial assistance options is crucial in alleviating this burden. Goggle Turn2Us to research available funding sources, such as local council grants or charitable organisations that may subsidise home care costs.

Additionally, create a detailed budget that outlines your income and expenses related to care. This will help you identify areas where you can allocate funds more effectively. Engaging with a financial advisor who specialises in disability benefits can also provide tailored advice to maximise your resources.

You can employ the support worker/carer/personal assistant of your choice, to take care of you. However, employing a PA means Registering with HMRC as an employer and registering personal assistants as employees, but you must pay your PA at least the National Minimum Wage; Calculating holiday pay entitlements and pay holiday payments. You are also required to manage employee sickness, check sick pay entitlements, and arrange sick pay; Calculate maternity and paternity leave and make required payments.

If you receive a Direct Payment card and employ a single full time carer, you are considered an employer and you would be responsible for your Carer in the same way, as you would expect your employment rights as a worker to be met by your employer.

Holiday pay and entitlement: Almost all workers are legally entitled to at least 28 days paid holiday per year. Your local council Direct Payment Support Services (DPSS) can calculate holiday entitlement and pay on your behalf. If you have any queries regarding holiday pay and entitlement you can contact adult social services and ask to speak with Direct Payment Support Services. You can also find out more about holiday pay and entitlement on the GOV.UK website.

The National Minimum Wage: is the minimum pay per hour almost all workers are entitled to. A worker's minimum wage depends on their age and whether they are employed as an apprentice. It's against the law for employers to pay workers less than the National Minimum Wage, or to falsify payment records.

Managing Carer sickness: If your employee cannot attend due to sickness, they should contact you as soon as possible. They should send you a medical certificate from a doctor (MED3 Statement of Fitness for Work from GP or MED10 from hospital) if their absence is likely to be longer than seven days. If the Statement of Fitness for Work says they 'may be fit for work', talk to your employee about possible changes that may allow them to return early, such as altering their hours or duties.

Statutory sick pay issues: Your employee might be entitled to Statutory Sick Pay (SSP). Find out more about SSP on the GOV.UK website.

Maternity and paternity pay and leave: All pregnant employees are entitled to take up to 52 weeks' statutory maternity leave around the birth of their child, where appropriate notice has been given. If an employee's partner is having a baby, they may also be eligible for paternity leave. You can get advice from us in managing maternity and paternity leave and pay, as there are legal procedures you must follow as an employer. You can find more information on both maternity and paternity leave and pay on the acas.org.uk website.

ACAS Helpline:
https://www.acas.org.uk/contact

Employing a carer can be tricky. The best way to manage your care is to find a carer through a private care agency, who manages all of the employment and tax issues for you. The Housing Care services directory can help you find online care homes and care agencies across the UK. You can search for care agencies on the following websites.

The Housing Care services directory:
https://www.nhs.uk/social-care-and- support/care-services-equipment-and-care-homes/national-homecare-providers/

Another option worth considering is to choose your own carer and negotiate your rate using an online care agency. Use a national care agency that you can join for free with no tie in contracts. Sign up and use the online platform to search for carer in your in local town or postcode, shortlist carers, contact and connect with background checked, qualified carers directly. You can find a carer and agree rates, hours and services that work for both of you The agency invoices you for the carer's visits, so you don't have to deal with employment and HMRC. Curam accept local authority payments, and you can also use your Direct Payment card and you only pay for the care that is delivered.

Find a Curam carer: Check out my website www.CareCoaching.co.uk for more information and a sponsored link to the Curam site..

You may decide to review your care package through a self directed package. If you decide you want to control your funding using a Direct Payment Card and your local council is currently making direct payments to your carer on your behalf, do not agree to stop direct payments until you receive your Direct Payment card.

Lastly, as a client and, or employer, understanding your patient rights in home care arrangements is vital for ensuring that your needs are met. Most people are unaware of their rights regarding privacy, dignity, and quality of care. You have a right to receive good service and care. It's important to learn about the relevant legislation and guidelines that protect these rights. This knowledge will empower you to advocate for yourself and make informed decisions about your care. Remember, you are not alone in the journey. A lot of people are going through a care crisis. With the right tools, support systems, and resources in place, you can become a satisfied client and successfully navigate the challenges of a Self-Directed assessment and create a fulfilling care plan that meets your needs.

Transitioning from hospital to home often bring

emotional challenges, including anxiety and uncertainty about recovery. It's important to acknowledge these feelings and seek support. It's important to get the right support quickly. The lack of home care to support the hospital-to-home transition is the number one cause of re-admissions of patients recently discharged from hospital. The first 72 hours after discharge from hospital stay is critical time for the patient. People often still require acute care, assistance with washing, changing and changes in daily routine, like medications, diet regimens, rehab activities, physiotherapy and more. Poor or non-existent care during this critical period can lead to serious complications. Connecting with local support groups or online communities can provide invaluable reassurance and advice from those who have faced similar experiences.

NHS Continuing Healthcare is a free package of care provided outside of a hospital environment for transitioning patients with complex healthcare needs, such as those with long- term conditions or disabilities. This care plan is fully funded by the NHS and is designed for people whose primary need is health-related rather than social care needs. NHS continuing healthcare is free, unlike care support provided by local authorities, which is means tested and involves the service users making financial contributions based on income and savings. The NHS funds your care package and the integrated care board (ICB) to decide the appropriate package of support. If you are assessed as eligible, you can receive NHS continuing healthcare in your own home, or in a care home. If you receive NHS continuing healthcare in your own home, the NHS will pay for your package of care and support to meet your assessed health and associated care needs, including a carer. If you are found to be eligible for NHS continuing healthcare in a care home, the NHS will pay for your care home fees, including board and accommodation.

If you currently have a local authority care package that is not meeting your needs and you wish to apply for a NHS Care package. Neither the NHS nor the local authority should withdraw from any existing care or funding arrangement without a joint reassessment of your needs, and without first consulting with one another, and with you, about any proposed change in arrangement, as well as ensuring that alternative funding or services are put into effect. The assessment for transitioning to NHS continuing healthcare should be at your home or care home. In the vast majority of cases, the checklist is completed when you are in a community setting. There may be rare circumstances where assessments may take place in the hospital environment. You will normally be given the opportunity to be present at the completion of the assessment checklist, together with any representative you may have.

If your health condition is critical and requires 24-hour attention after hospital discharge, or you believe your condition is palliative, or that you need specialist overnight care as well as daytime care, there may be another option to paying for local authority commissioned care. A NHS Continuing Healthcare package or personal health budget could better meet your assessed health and associated social care needs, if you meet the identified criteria in the NHS Continuing Care checklist.

NHS Continuing Care Assessments play a crucial role for patients navigating the complexities of post-hospital care, particularly for those in need of financial assistance for care who are homeowners, have a private pension, or need extra clinical support funded through personal independence payments and or similar benefits.

The NHS assessment is designed to determine whether an individual has acute ongoing healthcare needs that necessitate specialised support. If you or a loved one has been recently discharged from the hospital, understanding this process can empower you to advocate effectively for necessary services. Begin by familiarising yourself with the eligibility criteria used in these assessments, which focus on the level of care required, rather than solely on a diagnosis.
If you have a rapidly deteriorating condition and the condition may be entering a terminal phase, you may be eligible to receive urgent access to NHS continuing healthcare via fast track. In the fast track pathway there is no requirement to complete a checklist or the decision support tool. Instead, an appropriate clinician will complete the fast track pathway tool to establish your eligibility for NHS continuing healthcare. This

clinician will send the completed fast track pathway tool directly to your ICB, which should arrange for a care package to be provided for you, normally within 48 hours from receipt of the completed fast track pathway tool.

If you are eligible for NHS continuing healthcare, you would not undertake a Self-Directed Care Assessment as your ICB would be responsible for your care planning, commissioning services and your case management.

The ICB would discuss the options with you, as to how your care and support needs will be best provided for and managed. However, when deciding on how your needs will be met, your wishes and preferred outcomes should be taken into account. The NHS Continuing Care Assessment should include discussions about where you would receive the care (for example, at home or in a care home) as well as how your needs will be met and by who. The eligibility decision regarding NHS continuing healthcare should normally be made within 28 calendar days from the date the ICB received notification that of your request for NHS Continuing Care assessment.

If it turns out that you are not eligible for NHS Continuing Care, your next step is to initiate a Self-Directed Assessment. It is essential to lease with the ICB to get your Self-Directed Assessment process started. They will guide you through the necessary steps to request a care assessment tailored to your specific needs. The ICB can (with your permission) refer you to a local authority that can discuss with you whether you may be eligible for support from them. Even if you are not eligible for NHS continuing healthcare, but still have some health needs, then the NHS may still pay for part of your package of support. This is known as a 'joint package of care'. One way in which this is provided is through NHS-funded nursing care. The NHS might also provide other funding or services to help meet your needs.

If both the NHS and the council are involved in funding part of your care package then, depending upon your income and savings, you may have to pay them a contribution towards the costs of the local authority part of your care package. There is no charge for the NHS elements of a joint package of care.

Be prepared to provide detailed information about your health condition, daily activities, and how your recent hospital stay might have affected your overall well-being. This information will help assessors understand your unique situation and determine the level of support you require. Remember, the goal is to ensure you receive the right care to facilitate your recovery and enhance your quality of life at home.

How to Claim NHS Continuing Healthcare:
1. Assessment for NHS Continuing Healthcare:
If you have a significant and ongoing healthcare need, you may qualify for NHS Continuing Healthcare. The first step is to request an assessment. This can be done

through your Hospital discharge social worker, local NHS trust or GP.

2. Eligibility Criteria: You must meet certain eligibility criteria. These include having a primary health need (e.g., severe dementia, complex physical or mental health conditions). You can request a NHS Continuing Care assessment, especially if you are a patient being discharged from hospital. For help with requesting a NHS Continuing Care assessment visit the .Gov website or call the free Beacon help line on 0345 548 0300 for help. Integrated care boards, known as ICBs (the NHS organisations that commission local health services), must assess you. A team of healthcare professionals will carry out the assessment.

3. Receive a Decision and Care Plan: After the assessment, you will receive a decision about eligibility. If eligible, a care plan will be created, which may include living in a care home or receiving care at home.

4. Appealing a Decision: If you are not happy with the NHS Continuing Care assessment decision, the ICB letter explaining the decision should tell you how to appeal. If you're not happy with a Checklist decision you can ask the ICB to reconsider your case. If you're still unhappy, you can use the NHS complaints system to pursue your case. If you're not happy after a full assessment, you can ask the ICB to reconsider its decision.

Finding suitable home care and carers is a vital part of negotiating your self-directed care plan post-discharge. When seeking care, consider the skills and experience necessary to meet your individual needs. It's beneficial to look for care workers who specialises in your specific condition or have experience with elderly patients. During the interview process, ask potential candidates about their qualifications, previous experiences, and how they would handle particular challenges you may face. This not only ensures that your needs are met but also fosters a supportive relationship that can significantly impact your care and recovery.

Financial considerations are also a key aspect of navigating home care services. For those with savings above £23,250, self-funding care can be daunting, but there are various options to explore that can alleviate some of the financial burdens. Research local resources and organisations that may offer assistance or subsidies for home care services. Additionally, inquire about any grants or funding options through charities or local councils that support home care initiatives. Understanding how these financial avenues work can help you create a sustainable care plan while ensuring you receive the necessary support.

Finally, remember that transitioning from hospital to home can be a challenging process, but you are not alone. Engaging with family and friends for support and utilising community resources can greatly ease the transition. Emphasise the importance of mental health during recovery, as emotional support is just as vital as physical care. Encourage open communication with your care team and loved ones throughout this journey. By taking proactive steps and using all available resources, you can create a comprehensive care plan that promotes both recovery and independence in the comfort of your own home.

Sample Self-Directed Care Assessment Plan

A Self-Directed Assessment is all about giving you the power to control your own care. The process involves a thorough assessment of your needs and preferences, followed by the development of a care plan that allows you to choose how and where you receive care, as well as how it's paid for.

When creating a Self-Directed care assessment plan, the first step is to clearly identify your individual needs and preferences. Begin by evaluating your daily living activities and determining which tasks you find challenging or require assistance with. Create a plan. It does not have to be formal, think about it like a school project. Make a chart; use an A4 notepad if you like. It does not have to be perfect; you are not being graded on presentation. You plan just needs to be easy to read and to understand.

Consider all aspects of your daily routine, including personal care, household tasks, and social interactions. Documenting these needs will form the foundation of your assessment plan and help you articulate them when requesting support from care providers. This personalised approach ensures that the care you receive aligns closely with your lifestyle and preferences.

The Personal Touch – People usually want a photo of themselves (and possibly family) in their care plan, along with a short description of their likes, dislikes, and personality.

Accessible Formats – If you struggle with reading, visuals like pictures or drawings may be more effective in communicating care needs.

Tailored Presentation – You should be asked how they prefer their care plan to be presented, ensuring it reflects their personal preferences.

Visual Aids – Mind maps, speech bubbles, diagrams, and flow charts can help make care plans clearer and more user-friendly.

All About Me' Sections – Be inspired by care plans for people with learning disabilities or dementia, the about me section should be placed at the front and include all your important personal preferences.

Clear & Simple Language – Your care plan should be easy to understand, avoiding unnecessary jargon and structured in stages or sections for better readability.

Adaptability – Different audiences have different needs—professionals may require detailed medical information, while the care user will benefit from simpler, more personal versions of their care plan. The Care Plan Assistant app is a useful tool.

Next, it is essential to gather information on available home care services that cater to your specific requirements. Research local care agencies and independent care workers who specialise in post-hospital type care. Look for services that offer flexibility in scheduling and offer a range of support options, from companionship to specialised medical assistance. Utilise local community resources, online directories, and support groups to gather recommendations and reviews. These steps will empower you to make informed decisions about the care providers you consider for your assessment plan.

Once you have a list of potential care providers, the next phase involves reaching out to them to discuss your needs and assess their suitability. Prepare a list of questions that address their experience, training, and approach to care. Inquire about their availability, fees, and any additional services they might offer. It's also important to discuss your rights as a patient and ensure the providers are committed to respecting your preferences and dignity. This dialogue will help you gauge whether they align with your expectations and whether they can provide the level of care you need.

In developing your Self-Directed care assessment plan,

include a section dedicated to financial considerations. Review your budget and explore financial assistance options such as Personal Independence Payment or Disability Living Allowance.

Understanding your financial landscape will help you negotiate care services that fit within your budget while ensuring you receive the necessary support. If you are self- funding, be transparent with care providers about your financial situation; many are willing to tailor their services to accommodate varying budgets. Once your plan is ready you are ready for your assessment,

The Self-Directed ~Assessment Process - Step by Step:

1. Initial Assessment: You must specifically request a Self-Directed Care Assessment from the local authority. Do not agree to a Direct, or Directed Assessment. 'Self-Directed' means you want to be involved in planning your care. Once you have drafted a detail outline of your care needs. A care professional from your local council or another appropriate body will eventually conduct an assessment of your needs, either over the phone or in person.

2. Care Plan Development: You can draft a care plan before or during the assessment. This plan outlines what care and support you need and how you want to manage it.

3. Choosing Your Care: You'll have the option to

choose your own carers and decide where you receive care, whether in your home or elsewhere.

4. Payment Options: The assessment may lead to options such as Direct Payments or a Direct Payment Card to manage the cost of your care. These give you flexibility and control over how your care is delivered.

Finally, ensure that your Self-Directed care plan is not static but rather an evolving document that you can adjust as your needs change. Regularly review and update your plan, especially after any significant changes in your health or circumstances. Encouraging open communication with your care provider will foster a collaborative relationship, ensuring that your care continues to meet your needs effectively. By taking these proactive steps, you will not only enhance your comfort at home but also promote a sense of independence and well being during your recovery journey.

In the next chapter you will find out why the right home care and support worker is vital to the success of your care plan. Research local agencies that specialise in your specific condition, post-hospital care or seek recommendations from healthcare professionals. Ask potential caregivers about their experience, training, and approach to care. Choose a carer who not just meets your practical needs, but also respects your preferences and promotes your independence. Remember, this is your care journey, having a supportive and compatible caregiver can make all the difference in your recovery process.

03

Chapter 3: Finding the Right Home Care and Support Worker

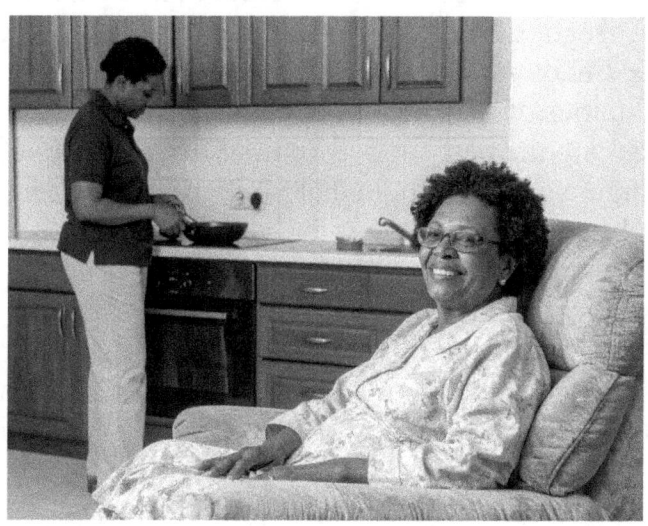

Choosing the right home care and support worker isn't just about ticking boxes—it's about finding someone who truly understands and respects your needs. The right person can make all the difference, bringing warmth, reliability, and a sense of security to everyday life. Whether it's about helping with daily routines, offering companionship, or providing essential care, a great carer or support worker is someone you can trust and feel comfortable with. On the flip side, the wrong fit can cause unnecessary stress, making things harder instead of easier.

This chapter dives into why getting the right match matters, what to look for, what to look out for and how to ensure the care you receive is supportive, compassionate, and the right fit for you.

Identifying Your Needs and Preferences
Identifying your needs and preferences is a vital first step in creating an effective care plan tailored to your unique situation. Whether you are navigating the complexities of personal independence payments or just seeking the best support options after a hospital discharge, understanding what you require is essential. Begin by reflecting on your daily routines, preferences, and challenges. Consider how your health condition impacts your ability to perform everyday tasks and what type of assistance will enable you to maintain your independence, dignity, and quality of life. This self-awareness will empower you as you embark on the journey of securing the right care.

Take time to assess your physical, emotional, and social needs. Are there specific activities you struggle with, such as bathing, cooking, or managing medications? Identifying the day-to-day challenges will help you articulate all your care requirements during the Self-Directed assessment process. Additionally, think about the emotional aspects of your care. Do you need companionship or support for mental health challenges? Recognising these needs can pave the way for a more holistic approach to your care, ensuring that every facet of your well-being is considered.

Your preferences also play an important role in shaping your care plan. Consider what kind of support worker would be the best fit for you. Do you prefer someone with specific training or experience? Would you feel more comfortable with a caregiver of a particular gender or background? It's essential that you outline these preferences as they will not only enhance your comfort but encourage a more productive working relationship with your support staff. Remember, the goal is to create an environment that feels safe and empowering for you. So you have to speak up.

As you work on identifying your needs and preferences, it can also be helpful to involve family members or friends in the discussion. They can provide valuable insights into your care requirements and help you articulate your needs more clearly. Additionally, they can assist you in finding quality home care and support services that align with your specifications. Engaging your support network ensures that you have a well-rounded perspective and reinforces your confidence in the decisions you make regarding your care.

Finally, as you gather this information and clarify your needs, keep in mind that resources are available to help you through this process. Creating the right care plan is hard work. Various organisations and support groups can provide guidance on navigating Self-Directed assessments and finding specialised home care services. By leveraging these resources, you can transition from hospital to home with the assurance that you have a comprehensive care plan in place, tailored specifically to your needs and preferences. Embrace this journey of self-discovery and empowerment; you are taking significant steps towards a more independent and fulfilling life.

Assessing Your Situation
For most people, some improvements to their care situation can be made. Along with poor health come lack of motivation and fuzzy thinking. Many people needing care may not have the vision, mental energy or concentration to read this book. As time goes on, the situation tends to worsen. The best time to read this book is when a health condition starts to deteriorate, and you are starting to think seriously about the possibility of support. Many people know what they don't like about their care, or care plan, but don't always correctly articulate their care needs. One way to figure out what changes need to be made is to create a health and wellness scoring system for your life.

First, list the areas of you life that affect you most:
Mobility
Pain
Spiritual/Religious
Mental well-being
Financial
Personal affairs
(Insurance, Funeral planning, wills etc.)
Work/Career
Physical exercise/Physiotherapy

Personal Relationships
Family/ Extended family
Friends/Social life
Help and Support

Next: Use a scoring system from 0 – 10 (with 10 being the optimal score, 0 meaning none existent and 1 meaning extremely poor) that reflects your personal satisfaction with your physical situation. Address each area briefly and give a score from 0 to 10 based on your feelings. You could do this exercise while you are making your care journal.

Look at these areas every day and make a score for each area in your journal. If the score frequently changes you may be feeling very emotional and may need to do the exercise on a weekly basis. If the Mobility, Pain, Spiritual/Religious, Mental Well-being, Physical Exercise/Physiotherapy, Personal Relationships, Family/ Extended Family, Friends/Social Life, Help and Support scores constantly fluctuate, there may be problems you are not addressing. Your scores may be based on treatment you received from a partner or carer. This may be based on their mood on a particular day. Your scores could also be based on your emotional feelings and mood. You may need new equipment, a better diet, supplementation, new carers, or therapy.

Below is an example of how you might lay out your **Total Health and Wellness Scoring System**

AREA	0 (LOW)	1	2	3	4	5	6	7	8	9	10 (HIGH)
Mobility		x									
Pain				x							
Spiritual/Religious							x				
Mental well-being							x				
Financial				x							
Personal Relationships								x			
Friends/Social life		x									
Personal affairs (Insurance, Funeral planning, wills etc.)					x						
Physical exercise/Physiotherapy		x									
Family/Extended family				x							
Help and Support			x								
Work/Career	x										

If you have very low scores in any area, you need to set care-needs goals for improvement. This is what is known as holistic health and improvement in any area can improve you health and well-being outcomes. The care plan and care assessment is an intrinsic part of creating and meeting those goals. If you have an acute, chronic or palliative health condition, then getting the right help, care and support is very important. Since you are reading this book, I imagine that in addition to your health and ability to cope alone or independently, there may be quite a few areas in your life that are causes for concern. Maybe you are concerned about your memory and your diet is becoming due to dysphasia or dementia. Maybe you are finding it difficult to get out of bed, or you are having a problem managing incontinence. Maybe you are cooped up indoor and would like to get out more, or perhaps you are simply receiving the wrong types of care for your needs. Whatever the problem is, by purchasing this book you are signalling that you are ready for a change. A successful care assessment will make a lot of difference to your care plan.

This guide may become a little repetitive on what I think are the important points. I will repeat myself, because there are a lot of people (like me) who tend to skip bits and jump to relevant sections. This book will explain how to find good carers, and if you are able to use a care plan assistant to app generate your personalised PDF Care Plan; you are on your way to a better care outcome.

Care Plan Assistant app: Check out www.CareCoaching.co.uk for free access

Using the Care Plan Assistant app can make a huge difference in your care assessment outcome. This comprehensive app is Care Act compliant and will take you through all the steps needed to create an enhanced care plan. It has form filed features that organise your personal information, care goals & outcomes, as well as your current support details, person-centred responses, and assessment preparation into a functional care plan that not only addresses your personal, care needs, but optimises your care hours and schedule to handle your personal nutritional, physical and social needs. The AI-generated routines, can also save chat responses, to create a structured weekly care plan with regional cost estimates based on your location. The comprehensive PDF plan generated is able to direct your assessment. Simply complete all the form sections and preview your plan before generating the plan to ensure all information is accurate. 'Once the forms are filled in, you will have everything you need to generate your own comprehensive care plan and direct your assessment with confidence. Just click on the 'Get Your Care Plan' tab.

Things To Consider When Making a Care Plan
A Care Plan is a record of what you aim to achieve during your recovery or in life. The care plan should record what your goals are, from your point of view.

People want their care plan to record and measures whether they are achieving their goals and recovering. Sometimes when people get involved in the creation of their care plans, they may set unrealistic goals. They are happy about what is in their plan but may not end up achieving their health and recovery goals or what the care plan said it would do. If the care plan does not achieve what it says it will do, then people tend to lose faith in the plan. Your care plan doesn't have to be like this. Deteriorating eyesight, dementia, brain fog, pain, depression, mental illness, learning disability and related conditions can affect a people's ability to read and retain and/or understand information. It is important that your care plan is accessible, simple, and easy to read and contains a good record of what has been agreed. Some care plans for people with learning disability use pictures and drawings to demonstrate goals. Care plans are supposed to make things better, so any care plan should make clear when the care plan will be reviewed, to see if it has made things better, and who will be involved in the review, and what observable change are expected to happen.

Being involved in your care plan is always better than leaving it to others—after all, no one knows your needs better than you do. The key is to be realistic, budget-conscious, and practical. A well-balanced plan should cover more than just your medical care. A good plan should also include diet, exercise, physiotherapy, social activities, fresh air, supplementation, and nutrition. Care is more than being washed changed and fed. Taking a holistic approach to your care plan ensures that the care you receive will support both physical health and overall well-being.
04

Chapter 4: Specialised Home Care for Elderly Patients

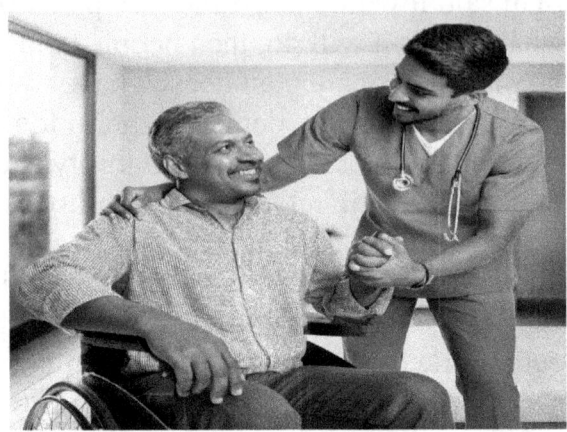

When someone we love starts to struggle with everyday tasks. When a simple walk to the kitchen feels like a marathon or managing medication becomes a daily puzzle. It gets heartbreaking.
We want to do everything to make life easier for our loved ones, but the truth is, caring for an Infirmed, disabled or elderly family member often requires more than just good intentions.

Specialised home care isn't just about assistance; it's about dignity, comfort, and making sure loved ones continue to feel safe and valued in their own home. Whether you're making the decision by yourself, or with family and loved ones, it's about finding the right support, someone who understands your needs, emotional well-being, and even the little quirks that make them who they are. Because in the end, it's not just about care—it's about peace of mind, for everyone.

Understanding Specialised Needs After Hospital Discharge

Understanding specialised needs after hospital discharge is crucial for ensuring a smooth transition back home. Everyone's individual experience in the hospital will differ significantly, which then leads to a variety of individual needs upon returning home. It is important to recognise that you may require additional support due to physical limitations, cognitive changes, or emotional distress. By identifying and understanding these specialised needs, you can create a tailored care plan that promotes independence and well-being.

The next step in addressing your specialised needs is to conduct a comprehensive assessment. The assessment usually involves an evaluation of your physical health, mobility, and daily living activities. If possible, involve healthcare professionals, such as occupational therapists or physiotherapists, who can provide insights into the specific requirements necessary for recovery. Additionally, family members should be consulted, as they often have a deeper understanding of your routine and preferences. By gathering this information, the assessment can be developed into a care plan that accurately reflects your individual needs.

As you navigate the Self-Directed assessment process consider researching and finding special resources that assist families in finding culturally competent home care options. Local community organisations, cultural centres, and online self help platforms often provide valuable information and support. These types of resources can connect you with caregivers who understand and respect the elderly, ensuring that you or your loved one receives care that aligns with your preferences. Engaging with these networks can also offer insights into funding options and financial assistance available for these types of care services, and help you make informed choices within your budge

Supporting mental health during care is another critical component that intersects with cultural care needs. As people get older their habits become set. Elderly people can often live in different era in terms of how they view others, and this may need sensitive handling. Cultural beliefs can often heavily influence how people perceive and manage mental health issues. Therefore, it is often essential to incorporate culturally appropriate mental health support into a care plan. Encouraging open, sympathetic discussions about emotional well-being, providing access to culturally relevant resources, and ensuring that caregivers are equipped to address these needs can significantly enhance the recovery experience. By recognising and prioritising cultural care needs, you will create a comprehensive care plan that nurtures the physical and emotional health for you or your loved one.

Finding the right home care and support worker is a vital part of this process. It is essential to look for caregivers who have experience in working with clients who have similar conditions or requirements. Conducting interviews and asking targeted questions can help ensure that the care worker's skills align with your needs.

Moreover, it is beneficial for you or your advocates to discuss the care giver's approach to care, their communication style, and availability. This not only builds trust but also fosters a supportive environment where everyone feels comfortable and understood.

Financial considerations can play a significant role in creating your care plan. For those receiving Personal Independence Payment (PIP), or similar types of financial assistance, understanding the available resources is key. Most people are not aware of the various funding options for home care services, which can alleviate some of the financial burden. It is advisable to research and explore local resources, charities, and government programs designed to support patients in need of home care after a hospital stay. By leveraging these resources, you and your families can make informed decisions that fit your budget while ensuring quality care.

Lastly, transitioning from hospital to home can have emotional implications that should not be overlooked. Supporting mental health during this transition is as important as addressing physical needs. Encouraging open communication about feelings and concerns can help you adjust more effectively.

You family should consider incorporating family social activities or counselling into the care plan to promote overall well-being. By taking a holistic approach to care that encompasses both physical and emotional health; families can ensure that loved ones thrive in their recovery journey.

Types of Specialised Home Care Services Available
When navigating the landscape of home care services, it's essential to understand the various specialised options available to meet your needs. Personal Independence Payment (PIP) recipients and those self-funding their care often require tailored services that align with their specific circumstances. Home care services can range from personal care assistance to specialised medical support, ensuring that patients receive the right level of care after a hospital discharge. You and your family can explore these options to create a care plan that not only addresses physical health needs but also supports emotional well-being during the transition back home.

The most significant type of specialised home care service is personal care assistance. This service focuses on daily living activities. This can include help with bathing, dressing, changing pads, grooming, and meal preparation. If you suffer with chronic or palliative conditions, or recovering from a debilitating illness or injury, having a compassionate caregiver to assist with these tasks can significantly enhance your quality of life. A good caregiver will often adapt their services to cater to your preferences and needs. The personalised approach fosters independence and dignity at home.

Another vital category of specialised home care is skilled nursing care. The District Nurse (DNS) and general practice nursing services, provide some free care services in the community. This service may be essential for individuals who require ongoing medical attention following a hospital stay, have a low budget and don't want personal care. Skilled nurses can administer medications, monitor vital signs, and provide treatments such as wound care.

Having a qualified healthcare professional at home alleviates some of the burden on family members while ensuring that the service user receive the medical oversight they need for a successful recovery. Your family should inquire about the qualifications and experience of nursing staff to ensure they find the right support for you.

If you are dealing with chronic conditions or cognitive

impairments, specialised home care services can also include rehabilitation therapy. Occupational, physical, and speech therapy can be provided in the comfort of your home, allowing you to regain your independence and improve your daily functioning. These therapies are designed to address specific challenges and can be tailored to the individual's pace and progress.
Engaging in therapy at home will usually enhance your motivation to do it regularly, as service users often feel more comfortable in their familiar surroundings.

Support for mental health is a crucial aspect of specialised home care services, particularly for patients who have recently been discharged from the hospital. Support services can include emotional support, companionship, and access to mental health professionals who offer counselling or therapy. Recovery is not just physical but also emotional. Understanding this helps you and your family to create the right care plan that addresses all aspects of well-being. By exploring different specialised home care options, your family can ensure you receive the best possible support during your recovery journey.

Choosing the Right Provider for Specialised Care

Choosing the right provider for specialised care is a crucial step in ensuring that you receive the support they need after being discharged from the hospital.

Therapy decisions can significantly impact recovery and overall well-being, so it's essential to approach the selection process with care and consideration. Begin by conducting thorough research on potential therapists and support workers, focusing on their qualifications, experience, and the specific services they offer. Look for providers who have a solid reputation and positive reviews from other families. Engaging with online communities or forums can also provide insights into the experiences of others in similar situations.

Once you have compiled a list of potential providers, it's important to assess their compatibility with your unique needs. Each person has distinct requirements based on their health conditions, preferences, and lifestyle. Just as you would discuss with a friend or family member, take the time to outline your needs and communicate them clearly to potential providers. This will help them in identifying staff that can tailor their services accordingly. Don't hesitate to ask about their approach to care, including their methods for promoting independence and dignity, as well as how they handle emergencies or unexpected changes in the client's condition.

Researching prospective care providers is a vital step in the selection process. Prepare a set of questions that cover key areas such as their training, experience with similar cases, and availability. It's also valuable to inquire about their approach to communication and how they involve family members in the care plan. During these interviews, pay attention to how the providers respond to your questions. A compassionate and attentive provider who demonstrates genuine interest in your well-being, and may even refer you to another agency that can make a significant difference in the quality of care received. In addition to evaluating the providers themselves, consider the logistics of the service arrangement. Discuss the financial aspects upfront, including whether they accept funding options that may be available, such as Direct Payments.

Understanding the costs involved will help in making an informed decision that aligns with your budget. It's also beneficial to ask about flexibility in scheduling and the option for trial periods, which can allow you to assess the fit before committing long-term.

Also, remember that the journey of recovery does not end with choosing your care providers. Continuous communication between carers, GP, care providers, therapists and the individual receiving care is essential for the ongoing assessment and adjustment of the care plan. . Regular check-ins can help identify any changes in your needs or preferences, ensuring that the support provided remains effective and responsive. By taking these steps and showing you are aware and observant, means you foster a collaborative relationship that prioritises your care needs and contributes to a smoother transition from hospital to home.

Meal planning can be especially important if you are a fussy eater, vegan, have food allergies and intolerances, or require a special or cultural diet. You may need to create a menu plan and find a carer that can prepare meals that you like. Council commissioned carers tend not to do much more than heat meals in the microwave. If you require more than this type of service, you may need to apply for direct payments and chose a suitable local carer through an online care agency

Direct Payments and Obtaining a Direct Payment Card

Direct payments offer a flexible and empowering way for individuals receiving various benefits, such as Personal Independence Payment (PIP) or Disability Living Allowance (DLA), to manage their own care and support. By opting for direct payments, you gain control over how your care is delivered, allowing you to tailor services to your unique needs, preferences, and circumstances. Direct payment can be especially beneficial for patients recently discharged from hospital, with mobility issues, as it enables these service users to choose the carers they are comfortable with and create a care plan that supports their recovery and enhances their quality of life. Understanding the process of obtaining a direct payment card is a crucial step in this journey. To begin the process, it's essential to request a Direct Payment Card during the Self-Directed assessment. You can initiate this by contacting your local authority or relevant organisation that handles care assessments. Direct Payment cards can take 8 weeks or longer to process. So changing to a Direct Payment Card after an assessment could cause a delay in the payments for your care services, which you may have to budget for.

During this assessment, be open about your needs and the type of support you envision for your post-hospital recovery. This is your opportunity to voice any specific preferences, whether that includes hiring a specialised home care worker or accessing particular services tailored to your situation.

Once your assessment is complete and you've been approved for direct payments, the next step is obtaining your direct payment card. This card functions like a debit card, allowing you to manage the funds allocated for your care directly. Your local authority will guide you through the application process, including setting up your account and understanding how to use the card. It's important to keep track of your spending and ensure that it aligns with the care plan you've created, as this will help you stay within your budget while meeting your care needs effectively.

As you navigate the complicated world of direct payments and managing your home care, it's a good idea to tap into the support networks. Many charities and organisations offer guidance and can connect you with others who have gone through similar experiences to yourself. Engaging with these communities can give you valuable insights and encouragement as you create a care plan that works for you. Remember, you are not alone in this journey; there are numerous resources available to support you.

05

Chapter 5: Assessing Individual Needs for Home Care Services

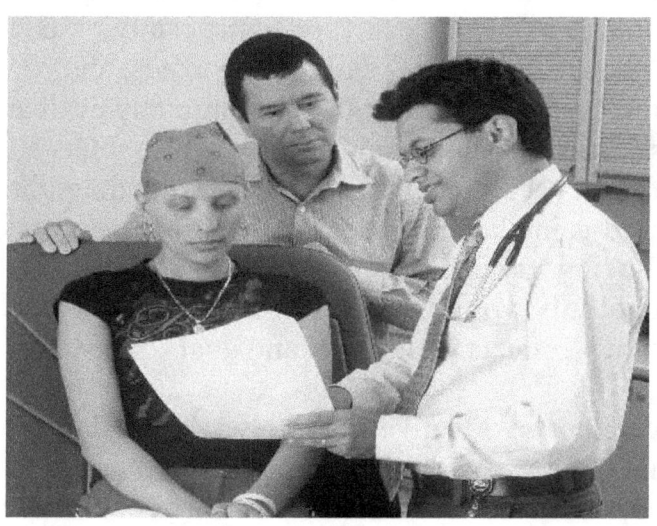

No two people age the same way. For some, it's little things—a misplaced set of keys, needing an extra hand with groceries. For others, it's more complicated, with mobility challenges or health conditions that make daily life tough. The truth is, there is no one-size-fits-all solution when it comes to home care and support. That's why taking the time to assess your individual needs is so important. It's not just about finding help; it's about finding the right help—the kind that fits like a glove and truly makes life easier, safer, and more comfortable. Because when support is personalised, it doesn't feel like an intrusion. It feels like care.

Conducting an Initial Needs Assessment

The initial needs assessment is a crucial step in creating a personalised care plan, particularly if you're a patient recently discharged from hospital. The process begins with understanding your unique requirements, which can vary significantly based on your health conditions, daily living needs, and personal preferences. Taking the time to thoroughly evaluate these aspects will not only facilitate a smoother transition back home but also ensure that the right support is in place to encourage your independence and well-being. By approaching your assessment thoughtfully, you can lay the foundation for a care plan that truly reflects your needs and goals.

To conduct an effective needs assessment, think like a social worker and start by gathering relevant information about your medical history, current health status, and any specific challenges they may face at home. This may involve consulting healthcare providers, reviewing discharge summaries, and discussing concerns with family members. It's important to consider both physical and mental health needs, as emotional well-being plays a significant role in recovery. Engaging in open conversations about you and your life will provide valuable insights and help identify areas where assistance is required, such as personal care, mobility support, or companionship.

Next, evaluate your living environment to determine if any modifications or accommodations are necessary to enhance safety and accessibility. Assess the layout of your home for potential hazards, such as stairs or narrow hallways, and consider the need for rails, stair climbers, assistive devices or other similar type home modifications. If you are struggling with living in areas of your home you may have to adapt your home.

In addition, monitoring your personal daily routines and activities, you can highlight specific times when care support may be essential, whether it's for meal preparation, or for carers using silicon food moulds for dysphasia, special meals medication management, sleep routines, or social activities. By taking all these factors into account, you can create a comprehensive picture of the kind of support that will be most beneficial.

Once you have gathered all the pertinent information, it's time to prioritise your identified needs. You will have to condense the time down into approximately 3-4 hours a day. This may involve using the Care Plan Assistant App, or simply collaborating with other family members to determine which areas require immediate attention and which can be addressed later. A well- prioritised needs assessment will not only streamline the care planning process but also ensure that the most critical needs are met promptly. Remember, the goal is to empower better health and create a sense of autonomy; these goals should guide the prioritisation process.

Finally, document the findings of your self-directed needs assessment clearly and concisely. The Care Plan

Assistant app generates a comprehensive care plan and care schedule. This documentation could be used to serve as a valuable reference for requesting a self-directed assessment, and during assessment.

Your local council will have a care needs eligibility criteria. If you have a normal assessment. Your care needs will be ranked in order of critical, substantial, moderate and low. With a self-directed care assessment, you needs are automatically incorporated with your critical and substantial needs.

Having a detailed account of your individual needs will facilitate informed discussions with the local authority and help ensure that the right support is secured for you. The process of creating a care plan might seem tedious, but remember that you are not alone and there are numerous resources available to assist you in finding the right home care and support to meet these needs

Involving Family in the Assessment Process
Involving family in the assessment process is crucial for creating a comprehensive care plan tailored for individual needs. Close friends and family members often have valuable insights into your daily routines, preferences, and challenges you face that may not be immediately apparent to you or the healthcare professionals. By actively engaging your family in the assessment and post-hospital care, you can help ensure your care plan reflects your medical, emotional and

social needs. A sense of shared family responsibility is sometimes what is needed to make it easier for everyone to get involved in supporting your care plan.

To begin involving family in the assessment process, you should initiate open and honest conversations about your condition and care requirements. Call family members and encourage them to express their observations and concerns, ask if they have noticed a specific issue that need addressing. This type of dialogue can help identify the types of support need you may have overlooked, whether that is assistance with a daily living activity, or getting some counselling or emotional support during recovery. By actively communicating with social services, families can work together to advocate for the best possible care options.

If you do involve your family in your care decisions, make sure their input is managed. When requesting a self-directed assessment, ensure that family members know their role in the process. They can help you gather relevant information, such as medical history and previous care experiences, which can be instrumental in shaping up a well-rounded care plan, but they don't have final say.

In addition, your family can assist you in identifying potential home care providers who align with your needs and preferences.

Once the assessment is underway, your family should remain engaged throughout the implementation of the care plan. Proactive involvement will not only enhance the assessment, regular check-ins can help ease the burden of care and monitor the effectiveness of the chosen services and allow for adjustments as necessary. This ongoing involvement reassures both you and family members that your needs are being met, and it fosters a very supportive environment for recovery. Furthermore, family feedback is great for evaluating home care workers, ensuring that they are a good fit and making sure that your care quality remains consistent.

I can't say this enough. The collaborative effort can lay the foundation for effective home care and empowers families to become active participants in the recovery journey. If you don't have family, get a Health and Wellness Coach. Embrace the opportunity to strengthen family bonds, and help others to learn the process for managing their own future care needs, which will enhance you overall care experience.

Prioritising Needs Based on Health and Lifestyle

Prioritising needs based on your health and lifestyle is a crucial step in creating a care plan that effectively supports you after a hospital discharge. Understanding your unique circumstances and health requirements will enable you to identify the right resources and support services tailored to your situation. Begin by assessing your current health status and any limitations that may affect your daily activities. The Care Plan Assistant App works great for this task. This evaluation helps you determine the assistance you need right now, whether its help with personal care, mobility support, medication management, or emotional support.

Once you have a clear picture of your health needs, consider how your lifestyle factors into the equation. Lifestyle encompasses your normal daily routines, social activities, and personal preferences, all of which play a significant role in your recovery and overall quality of life. Work on a care plan that prioritises your needs by creating a list that ranks them according to urgency and importance. Start with the essential tasks, such as personal hygiene and medication management, followed by activities that support your emotional health, like social interaction and hobbies. For instance, if you enjoy gardening or reading, planning your care around resuming these activities can enhance your mental well-being. Be prepared to discuss how a carer could support you to continue these activities.

This prioritisation will help you communicate effectively with your care providers, ensuring your healthcare providers focus on what matters most to you. When you articulate your needs clearly, it becomes easier to find a caregiver who aligns with your expectations and can offer the specific support required care journey.

As you navigate the process of requesting a self-directed assessment, be proactive about discussing your priorities with the assessment team. They are supposed to help you, so don't hesitate to voice your needs and preferences. This dialogue can lead to better-tailored services that align with your health and lifestyle goals. Additionally, you can utilise resources such as local support groups or online forums can provide valuable insights and recommendations from others who have been through similar experiences, ensuring you are well-informed while making decisions.

As your health journey changes, or your recovery progresses, your care needs may change, necessitating adjustments to your care plan. Care plan are usually reviewed after 6 months. Regularly re-evaluate your situation and communicate any changes in your needs to your caregiver or support team. Staying engaged in your care plan allows you to advocate for yourself effectively and ensures you receive the right level of support, Embrace this journey, knowing that your care is an ongoing process and with the right approach and support, you can maintain a decent lifestyle.

The conventional care needs assessment usually involves a visit from someone from your local council such as a social worker or occupational therapist. They will usually ask you how you're managing everyday tasks like washing, dressing and cooking. They might ask you to describe how well you do certain things like making a cup of tea and getting out of a chair. The care assessment is supposed to cover the key issues, but the people doing the assessment can only make notes about 'presenting needs' – which means the needs that are mentioned during the needs assessment itself. If they forget to ask about something important and you don't bring it up, it won't be included in the care plan. People often downplay or neglect to mention their real day-to-day needs and difficulties during assessments and this can affect the level of support they're entitled to.

Self-Directed support helps the people who use social care to take much greater control over their care. Self-Directed care works by using a combination of direct payments, individual budgets and council commission care agencies and succeeds best by making sure that beforehand there is complete list made of all the issues and difficulties the service user is facing, to ensure nothing is forgotten. Every little thing should be documented, who cuts your fingernails, how many cups of tea a day you need, hair dressing, cultural food items and where they can be purchased, what time you get up in the morning, going outside, allergies, languages spoken, over the counter medication and supplements, what type of music you like, social activities.

There are 4 Options for Self-Directed support

Option 1 - a direct payment, which is a payment to a service user, or third party to purchase his or her own support.

Option 2 - the service user directs how the available support is used and portioned out, part privately arranged and part council commissioned.

Option 3 - the local council arranges all the support.

Option 4 - a mix of the above.

Self-Directed Support assessments are great, because you can combine council commissioned care workers, with private carers funded by direct payments. If you receive Direct Payments, the council will either deduct the amount of your contribution to care before the direct payment is made, or will make the direct payment in full and you will have to reimburse your contribution. However, if you are eligible to receive Direct Payments, the most your contribution to care costs can be is £100.00 a week. But there are a few caveats, you have to spend all the money, or you will have to pay the council back any unspent amount. If you don't use an agency, on average, the council will offer to pay about £16.00 per hour for you to employ a private carer who can be paid up to £12.39 per hour. The remainder of the hourly rate (£3.61) will be expected to cover all other costs associated with employing of Personal Assistants including; payroll, sick pay, holiday pay, pension and renewal of insurance and the costs of hiring another carer from an agency, while your usual carer is sick or on holiday.

Often Direct Payments are not enough to buy services to meet your needs. The council will pay a higher rate for the personal care and support services that you need and you can receive the remainder in Direct Payment funds for funding other types of care and social activity. Another good thing about the Self-Directed Assessments is that you can split your care hours between council commissioned and private agencies care. The council is willing to spend up to £25 per hour, for agency staff, and are willing to spend on double up care with their own council commissioned care agencies. So you might want to consider using council commissioned carers for personal care like morning and evening washing, bathing and changing.

Understanding Cultural Care Needs

Understanding cultural care needs is essential for providing effective and compassionate support to care users, especially the elders.

Every person carries unique cultural backgrounds that shape their values, beliefs, and preferences regarding health and care giving. Recognising these differences not only enhances the quality of care but also fosters trust and rapport between clients and caregivers. As you embark on creating your care plan, consider how cultural factors influences the way you perceive your health and the kind of assistance you desire.

When assessing your need for home support services, it is crucial for the assessor to engage in open and respectful dialogue with everyone involved. The conversation should explore your cultural practices and preferences, such as dietary restrictions, you personal communication styles, and what the level of family involvement in making care decisions, will be.
Taking the time to understand all the issues around care

helps in tailoring services that resonate with your age, identity, background and ensure you feel respected and valued. A culturally competent approach significantly enhances the effectiveness of the care package provided, and will promote better health outcomes.

Finding specialised home care for elderly patients after hospital discharge can be challenging, particularly when cultural needs are involved. So it is vital to seek home care workers who not only qualified but also demonstrate cultural sensitivity and awareness. During the interview process, don't forget to ask potential caregivers about their experiences in working with the elderly, diverse racial backgrounds and their strategies for accommodating different cultural beliefs. This can help you identify caregivers who are well-suited to meet the specific needs of you or your loved one, and contribute to a smoother transition into care.

Another thing I should mention is, to try to find good carers and support before you have an assessment. A major cause of hospital readmission is stress and strain. Getting help and care before you reach a point where you really need help is sometimes the best thing you can do for yourself. It's not a luxury. While you're recovering, invest in some home care for 1-2 hours a week, for things like cleaning, support with going out for walks, or socialisation, or even someone to talk to. Therapy can improve health dramatically and aid in recovery. It's important if you have a memory condition like early onset dementia, to start your relationship with a carer early, before you have to find a carer urgently. Having multiple carers carrying out very personal tasks can be very distressing for most, and knowing your carer and building a rapport can make any future daily personal care tasks more pleasant.

Taking Control of Negative Care Assessment

What do you do if you have had an assessment and the outcome was not as expected? Understanding your rights and the appeals process under the Care Act 2014 is crucial to ensuring you receive the care and support you need. The following information is to guide you through the steps for disputing a care assessment decision and provides the necessary resources to quickly expedite your appeal, if you are not happy with your assessment.

The Care Act 2014

The purpose of the Care Act is to ensure that peoples' well-being is at the heart of care and support services. Some of its key principles centre on:

- promoting well-being
- preventing, reducing and delaying needs, and
- providing information and advice

Care Act appeals

You can appeal decisions related to:

- eligibility for care and support
- assessment and review outcomes

- care and support plans

You might appeal a Care Act decision for several reasons, such as:

- **disagreement with an assessment**
  if you believe the assessment of your strengths and care needs is incorrect or incomplete

- **eligibility disputes**
  If you have been deemed ineligible for certain services or care and support that you believe you need

- **Care Fees**
  The process for appealing against a financial assessment can be found in the local auth Financial Charging Policy in their .Paying for Care' guidance.

- **inadequate care and support**
  if the care and support plan provided does not:
    - build on your strengths,
    - enable you to engage with your community
    - prevent, reduce, or delay your needs, or
    - does not meet your needs

If you're preparing for a local authority care assessment or challenging a care plan that doesn't meet your needs — this worksheet is your ally.
Too often, care applicants are dismissed, delayed, or denied the support they're entitled to. You may have to

push back with clarity, confidence, and evidence to uncover the systemic and intersectional barriers and document your unmet needs and the procedural failings that led to you being denied care.

Whether you're requesting a reassessment, submitting a formal complaint, or preparing for a care review meeting, you must speak with the local authority and demand accountability. Your voice matters. Your care needs matter. So make sure they're heard.

Think about the assessment process and create a personal questionnaire. Ask yourself questions like:
- *What support have you requested but been denied?*
- *Were your concerns dismissed or minimized during meetings?*
- *Have you struggled to get clear answers or accountability from your care coordinator or local authority?*
- *What impact has inadequate care had on your well-being, independence, or safety?*
- *Have language barriers affected your ability to communicate your needs or understand your care plan?*
- *Have you faced discrimination or bias due to disability, race, gender, or other identity factors?*
- *Have cultural differences been acknowledged*

and respected in your care planning?

- *Have you had difficulty accessing interpreters, translated materials, or culturally appropriate services?*
- *Have you felt excluded or misunderstood because of your background or lived experience?*
- *What additional support would help you feel heard, respected, and included in care decisions?*

Create a scoring system to quantify the severity and frequency of the barriers you're facing.

Here's how the scoring system works:

- Each answer is paired with a **1–5 scale**:
    - **1 = Not at all**
    - **2 = Rarely**
    - **3 = Sometimes**
    - **4 = Often**
    - **5 = Very often or severely**

You can use you score to identify which issues are the most urgent. Prioritise what to rise in review meetings or complaints and spot patterns that may indicate systemic failings.

Suggested Next Steps Based on Questionnaire Scores

Next step is to align your issues with the statutory thresholds under the Care Act 2014. It will help you interpret your questionnaire scores and take action with confidence.

Scores of 1–2 *Monitor and document.* These areas may not require immediate action but should be tracked in case conditions worsen or patterns emerge.

Scores of 3–4 *Raise concerns in your next care review.* Prepare examples and evidence. These scores suggest recurring issues that may be impacting well-being or independence.

Scores of 5 *Take assertive action.* These may indicate serious unmet needs or statutory breaches. Consider:

- Requesting a reassessment under **Section 9** of the Care Act
- Challenging your care plan under **Section 25**
- Submitting a formal complaint or escalating to the **Local Government and Social Care Ombudsman**
- Seeking support from an independent advocate under **Section 67**, if you face substantial difficulty participating

Next create a checklist-style action plan to turn your reflection into assertive next steps. A checklist will help you move from identifying barriers to taking strategic action, especially when your scores indicate statutory breaches or serious unmet needs.

Here's what your checklist should include

✓ Checklist-Style Action Plan
Based on Your Scores:

- [ ] Review your questionnaire and highlight answers with scores of **3 or higher**
- [ ] Flag any scores of **5** and note the specific issues they relate to
- [ ] Gather supporting evidence (e.g. emails, care records, meeting notes) for high-scoring concerns
- [ ] Draft a summary of your **top 3 areas of concern**
- [ ] Decide whether to raise these in your next care review or submit a **formal complaint**
- [ ] Use the **sample letter templates** to structure your appeal or adjustment request
- [ ] Consider requesting a **reassessment under Section 9** of the Care Act 2014
- [ ] If facing substantial difficulty participating, request an **independent advocate under Section 67**
- [ ] Reach out to **local advocacy groups or legal support services**
- [ ] Track responses and follow-up actions in your workbook

Constructing your checklist in this way makes it easier to articulate the issues. This format makes it easy to write letters, annotate, or share information with advocates and care coordinators. Once you completed your questionnaire and checklist, you are ready for appeal

Initial Steps For Raising Concerns

Before making a formal appeal, try to resolve the issue informally by discussing your concerns with the social care worker or their Team Leader and keep detailed records of all communications and decisions.

Formal Appeal Process

You have the right to appeal many care decisions made by Adult Social Care under the Care Act 2014. The appeals process is supposed to ensure transparency and provides a straightforward way for you to contest decisions you believe are unfair or incorrect.

You Can Appeal Decisions Related To:

- **Assessment of needs**: Whether your needs have been accurately assessed
- **Carer's assessment**: Whether the assessment of your role as a carer is accurate
- **Eligibility decision**: Whether you qualify for support, or the level of support provided
- **Financial assessment**: Whether the financial assessment is accurate and considers all relevant information

- **Support planning**: Whether your care plan meets your needs and wishes

- **Personal budgets and direct payments**: Whether the allocated funding is sufficient

What You Cannot Appeal:
- Issues unrelated to Adult Social Care decisions or actions
- Matters already subject to legal proceedings
- Concerns the local authority feels might be better addressed through the Adult Social Care complaints policy, such as staff behaviour, delays, or communication issues

The Adult Social Care appeals policy follows a 2-step process.

Step 1: Early (Informal) resolution
- You should discuss your concerns with your allocated worker as soon as possible
- The allocated worker will review the decision and consider any additional information to try and resolve the issue quickly
- This informal discussion should happen promptly, with the goal of resolving issues by the next working day if possible

Step 2: Review and decision
- If early resolution is not possible, a formal appeal can be made within **15 working days** of receiving the decision
- You must submit your appeal within four weeks of receiving your completed assessment, review or care and support plan.
- Appeals can be submitted **online, by letter, email, or phone**
- Appeals should be acknowledged within **3 working days**
- A Service Manager will review the appeal, considering all available information.
- If necessary, a meeting may be arranged to discuss the appeal in further detail
- The Service Manager will provide a final decision within **15 working days** of receiving the appeal

How to Submit an Appeal
Appeals can be submitted by:
- Online form
- Sending an email or letter addressed to the Adult Social Care manager at your local council

You will need to provide:
- Your contact details
- Details about the decision you are appealing
- Any additional supporting information

Additional support and resources
If you remain dissatisfied, you can request for an advocate to help with using your local authority **Adult Social Care complaints procedure, or** contact the Local Government and Social Care Ombudsman.

Advocacy Services
If you cannot represent yourself, you have the right to an advocate who can support you through the appeals process.

Legal Advice
Consider seeking your own legal advice if your appeal is complex.

Support Organisations
Contact organisations like:
- Age UK
- Mencap, or
- Citizens Advice

for additional support and guidance

Key contacts

- Local Government and Social Care Ombudsman
  PO Box 4771
  Coventry
  CV4 0EH
  Telephone: 0300 061 0614
  Website: www.lgo.org.uk/contact-us
-
- Advocacy Services
  PO Box 375
  Hastings
  East Sussex
  TN34 9HU
  Email: info@theadvocacypeople.org.uk
  Telephone: 0330 440 9000
  Website: www.theadvocacypeople.org.uk

06

Chapter 6: Resources for Families Seeking Home Care

Between doctor visits, medication schedules, and daily support, it's easy to feel stretched thin. And while we want to do everything possible to make sure we're safe and comfortable, the reality is that care often comes at a cost. That's where government funding and resources can make all the difference. Whether it's financial support, access to specialised programs or simply guidance on where to start, these resources aren't just helpful—they're lifelines. Because when families are given the right tools, caring for a loved one doesn't have to feel like an impossible balancing act. It can be something sustainable, something that truly works.

Government and Non-Profit Resources

Government and non-profit resources play a crucial role in supporting individuals navigating the complexities of Self-Directed assessments and home care services. For those claiming Personal Independence Payment (PIP), New Style Employment and Support Allowance (ESA), or other related benefits, understanding the available resources can empower you to make informed decisions about your care. Various government programs are designed to assist people in assessing their needs, obtaining financial support, and connecting with the right home care services. It's essential to explore these options to ensure that you receive the assistance you deserve during your recovery.

Local councils often provide information and support for patients seeking home care services after being discharged from the hospital. They can help you understand what services are available in your area, including the specifics of self-directed assessments. By reaching out to your local council, you can gain insights into available funding options, eligibility criteria, and the process of requesting a self- directed assessment. Additionally, they can guide you in selecting appropriate care providers and help you assess your individual needs based on your unique circumstances.

In addition to government resources, numerous non-profit organisations offer valuable assistance and guidance. These organisations often have a dedicated team of staff, who are knowledgeable about the various benefits, services, and support systems available to individuals with disabilities and their families. They can provide information on how to navigate the complexities of home care, help you understand your rights, and connect you with specialised home care providers. Engaging with these non-profits can also give you access to community support networks, which can be immensely beneficial during your transition from hospital to home.

When it comes to financial assistance, there are several funding options available for those who may need to self-fund their care. Many organisations provide information about grants and subsidies that can ease the financial burden of home care services. Researching these options and discussing them with your care team can lead to discovering valuable resources that may not be immediately apparent. Additionally, understanding how to budget effectively can help you maximise the resources you have while ensuring you receive the necessary support for your recovery.

Take advantage of the resources available to help you evaluate and interview potential home care workers. Many organisations provide guidelines and best practices for assessing the qualifications and compatibility of caregivers. This process is critical in ensuring you find someone who not only meets your care needs but also aligns with your preferences and values. By utilising government and non-profit resources, you can confidently create a personalised care plan that supports your recovery and enhances your quality of life at home.

What Is Preventative Care & Recovery Coaching?

Preventative Care & Recovery is a form of support, provided by skilled and experienced health care workers, that helps you to manage pain and maintain your mobility, through regular physical activities and healthcare, nutrition and social connection. Preventative care and support can make a big difference. Especially f you are worried about maintaining your home, getting back into employment, avoiding readmission after leaving residential care, or being discharged from hospital.

Support Workers and Link Officers can help clients who are recovering after mental or physical trauma, hospitalisation, and or chronic illness, to become free from pain and find their passion, so that they actually want to wake up morning, restart their life, find new goals and get back to work. They do this by taking you through proven systems, step-by-step.

If you worried about maintaining your home, getting back into employment, avoiding readmission after leaving residential care, or being discharged from hospital? A good wellness and care coaching program can provide personalised support you need, with food plans, solutions for shopping, video communications, PA services, sourcing physiotherapy and carers, mobility equipment, while convalescing or adapting to a disability, so that you can feel like yourself again.

You might be wondering, "Can recovery coaching really make a difference?" The answer is yes. A skilled and experienced coach can help you access the necessary resources, take positive action, and rebuild a fulfilling and healthier lifestyle. The CareCoaching site provides guidance for making the right care plan and the best recovery options, to help overcome obstacles and achieve long-term success in your health journey.

Health and wellness coaching is great for care users, with one or more long-term conditions, who want to improve their lifestyle; or carers, who need support with caring and their caring roles, deal with stress, fatigue or mental health issues. Or those who are lonely or isolated, or who have complex social needs that affect their well-being. I'm a care coach and if you want to find out more about Health and Wellness Coaching you can check out my website at: www.carecoaching.co.uk

Online Tools and Platforms for Finding Care
In today's digital age, various online tools and platforms have emerged to assist you and your family in finding the right care solutions tailored to your specific needs. For those navigating the complexities of Self-Directed assessments and looking for home care support after a hospital discharge, these resources are invaluable. They can help you identify care options that align with your budget while ensuring that you

receive the necessary support. Whether you are seeking assistance for yourself or a loved one, searching and using these online tools can make the search for care more manageable and efficient.

One of the most effective platforms available is the UK Government's official website (*.Gov*), which provides comprehensive information on the Personal Independence Payment (PIP) and other benefits. This resource not only outlines eligibility criteria but also offers guidance on how to request a Self-Directed assessment. By understanding your rights and the available financial assistance, you can better navigate the funding options for home care services. Additionally, the .Gov platform connects you with local councils and health services, ensuring you have access to the most relevant information for your situation. You can find a list of Community support groups and organisations at https://www.gov.uk/find-a-community-support-group-or-organisation

Social media groups and online forums are a valuable resource for connecting with others who are in similar situations. These communities often share personal experiences; recommendations for home care workers, and practical tips for managing care at home. Engaging with others in online forums can provide emotional support, feedback and insights into local service providers who have been vetted by others who have used them. Asking questions and sharing your own experiences can enhance your understanding of what to look for in your care support.

Dedicated websites that specialise in home care services can simplify the process of finding qualified care workers. These platforms typically allow you to filter potential caregivers based on specific criteria, such as experience with elderly clients or familiarity with post-hospital care. Many of these sites provide user reviews and ratings, which can help you assess the quality of care offered by different agencies or individual caregivers. Taking the time to read through these reviews can build your confidence in selecting the right support for yourself or a loved one.

Online assessment tools can really help you evaluate your individual needs and preferences for home support services. These tools often guide you through a series of questions to determine the level of care required, allowing you to create a personalised care plan. By leveraging these resources, you can make informed decisions about your care options, ensuring a smoother transition from hospital to home. Remember, you are not alone in this journey; with the right tools and resources, you can find the support necessary to thrive in your home environment.

What is NHS Continuing Healthcare and How to Claim It?

NHS Continuing Healthcare (CHC) is a comprehensive package of care provided outside of hospital settings for those with significant ongoing healthcare needs. This care package is funded entirely by the National Health Service (NHS) and is designed for those who require extensive medical care, support, and supervision due to their health conditions. If your medical condition is unstable and/or unpredictable and you need constant 24 hour supervision, monitoring or specialist/acute nursing care, you may be eligible to received NHS Continuing Healthcare. The National Framework document sets out the process for establishing eligibility for Continuing Healthcare. To qualify for NHS Continuing Healthcare, you must meet the specific NHS eligibility criteria, which involves a thorough assessment of your health and care needs. This support can cover a range of services, including personal care, nursing care, and other essential support, ensuring that you receive the assistance you require to live comfortably at home

Claiming NHS Continuing Healthcare begins with the initial assessment, which can be initiated by a healthcare professional, such as a nurse or doctor, or by the individuals themselves. It is vital to gather all pertinent medical records, prescriptions and documents that outline your health conditions and care needs. Once the initial assessment indicates potential eligibility, a multi-disciplinary team will conduct a more detailed assessment. This team will evaluate your needs across various domains, including mobility, nutrition, and psychological well-being. Understanding the process is crucial, as it empowers care users and their families to advocate for the support they need.

If you or a loved one has recently been discharged from the hospital and you are considering applying for NHS Continuing Healthcare, it's important to be well-prepared. Start by compiling a comprehensive care plan that outlines all your healthcare needs and preferences. This plan should highlight any specialised home care services that may be required, especially if there are specific medical conditions involved. Use the Care Assistant App. Also ask if there are any resources available within the community that can provide additional support, for your specific care needs, which may range from accessing local advocacy groups, to connecting with specific healthcare professionals experienced in navigating the NHS system.

Community Support and Advocacy Groups
Community support and advocacy groups play a crucial role for people navigating the complexities of care. These groups serve as vital resources, providing information, assistance, and camaraderie to those applying for Personal Independence Payment (PIP) or other financial support. By connecting with these organisations, you can gain insights into the Self-Directed assessment process, which is essential for tailoring care to your specific needs. Whether you are a client or a caregiver, Community support and advocacy groups can empower you to advocate for your rights and secure the assistance necessary for a smooth transition back home.

One of the significant benefits of community support groups is the wealth of shared experiences and knowledge they offer. Members often share personal stories; their strategies for successful assessments, and tips for finding qualified home care workers. Their collective wisdom can help you feel less isolated and more informed about the options available. Many advocacy organisations also provide workshops or informational sessions that delve into how to request a Self-Directed assessment, ensuring you have all the tools necessary to navigate the system confidently. The Care Plan Assistant App is another useful tool.

In addition to offering information, these groups often provide direct support in finding specialised home care for elderly clients or individuals with specific needs. They often maintain directories of vetted home care providers, ensuring that you can find someone who meets your unique requirements. Many advocacy groups also collaborate with local services to help facilitate introductions between clients and caregivers, making it easier to find the right fit for your post-hospital care. This support can be invaluable for you to assess individual needs and make decisions about the care plan that will work best for you or your loved one.

Financial assistance is another critical area where community support can make a significant difference. Many advocacy groups are well-versed in the various funding options available for home care services, including navigating the complexities of PIP, ESA, and DLA.

Specialised organisations can guide you through the process of applying for benefits, and ensure you know your rights and entitlements. With their help, you can explore additional financial resources, such as grants or local assistance programs that can help alleviate the burden of self-funding care when on a budget.

Lastly, advocacy groups often emphasise the importance of mental health during the recovery process. Transitioning from hospital to home can be challenging, and the emotional support that community groups provide cannot be overstated. They create a reasonably safe space for discussing your fears, anxieties, and hopes for recovery, they allow both caregivers and service users alike to share their feelings and receive encouragement. A lot of people discover that these services are lifeline. By fostering close connections and promoting mental well-being support, these advocacy organisations not only assist with practical matters but also contribute to the overall mental health and happiness of care users during their recovery journey.

Below is a list of charities and organisations that may be able to support you or help you find care that suits your needs or give you advice on disability or health.

Care Regulators
Care Quality Commission (CQC) – Regulates and inspects care services in England to ensure high standards.

Care Inspectorate Wales (CIW) – Oversees social care and childcare services in Wales, ensuring quality care.

Care Inspectorate (CI) – Scotland's care regulator, inspecting care homes and nursing facilities for quality.

Care England – Represents care providers, including care homes and voluntary organisations.

Care Forum Wales – Supports health and social care providers in Wales.

Care Rights UK – offers advice on care services, costs, and policy.

Regulation and Quality Improvement Authority (RQIA) – Monitors and inspects health and social care in Northern Ireland.

Action for M.E. – Supports individuals with M.E./CFS through advice, helplines, and online forums.

Charities & Organisations
Age UK – Provides services, advice, and support to improve life for older people.

Alzheimer's Research – Funds research to find a cure for Alzheimer's and dementia.

Alzheimer's Society – Supports dementia care and research, offering help lines and local resources.

Arthritis Action – Helps people manage arthritis through advice, nutrition, and clinical support.

Bipolar UK – offers peer support groups, forums, and help lines for those affected by bipolar disorder.

BRACE – Funds dementia research for earlier diagnosis and better treatments.

British Deaf Association – Supports the deaf community with advocacy, advice, and sign language courses.

BILD – Promotes good practices for supporting people with learning difficulties.

British Society of Gerontology – Advances research and education on ageing

Cancer Research UK – Funds cancer research and provides support services.

Care Workers Charity – Provides financial and mental health support for care workers.

Carers UK – Supports unpaid carers through advice and help lines.

Cinnamon Trust – Helps older or terminally ill people care for their pets.

Citizens Advice – Provides guidance on financial and legal matters.

Cruse Bereavement Care – Supports people coping with grief and bereavement.

Dementia UK – offers advice and emotional support through specialist nurses.

Hearing Dogs for the Deaf – Trains dogs to alert deaf individuals to important sounds and provides UK-wide support groups.

Independent Age – offers financial guidance, grants, and free advice for older adults. Helpdesk: helpdesk@hearinglink.org Tel: 01844 348111

Hourglass – Supports older people facing abuse (physical, psychological, financial, sexual, or neglect). 24/7 Help line: 0808 808 8141

Diabetes UK – Provides resources, forums, and help lines for managing diabetes.

Disability Rights UK – Advocates for disability rights and policy improvements.

Friends of the Elderly – offers care homes, respite care, and financial aid for older adults.

Headway – Supports people with brain injuries through advice and emergency funding.

Young Dementia Network – Provides resources for those with young-onset dementia.

Cancer & Chronic Condition Support

Macmillan Cancer Support – Provides emotional, practical, and financial cancer care. Support Line: 0808 239 1492

Macular Society – offers advice on macular disease for individuals and families. Help line: 0300 3030 111

Marie Curie – Provides hospice care and emotional support via Marie Curie nurses. Support Line: 0800 090 2309

Mencap – Supports individuals with learning disabilities through guidance and forums. Help line: 0808 808 1111 | helpline@mencap.org.uk

Parkinson's UK – Provides advisors for medical and financial support. Help line: 0808 800 0303

Stroke Association – Supports stroke survivors with research and peer groups.

Mental Health & Disability Advocacy

MIND – offers confidential mental health help and legal advice.

Re-engage – Reduces loneliness for older adults via social activities and call companions.

Samaritans – Provides 24/7 support for anyone struggling emotionally. Help line: 116 123

Scope – Advocates for disability rights and offers practical advice. Scottish Care – Represents independent social care providers in Scotland.

Care Organisations & Support Networks National Care Association – Supports small and medium-sized care providers.

National Care Forum – Represents not-for-profit care organisations and advocates for policy improvements.

National Care Help line – Provides guidance on care options. Help line: 0800 0699 784

Skills for Care – Enhances social care workforce training and standards.

07

Chapter 7: Creating a Care Plan & Getting The Most Out of Your Care Needs Assessment

"Information, information, information – without it, how can people be truly at the heart of decisions? Information should be available to all regardless of how their care is paid for. There are some things that should be universal – information is one."

Public response to the Caring for our future engagement

ITEMS IN CARE PACKAGE	COUNCIL CARE ASSESSMENT	TOTAL HOURS (per week)	SELF-DIRECTED ASSESSMENT	TOTAL HOURS (per week)
Washing/changing/dressing	√	18	√	14
Shopping	√	0.5	√	1
Wash comb hair	√	0.5	√	1
Physiotherapy	✗	0	√	1
Household cleaning	√	1	√	1
Laundry	√	2	√	2
Outings	✗	0	√	2
Cooking	✗	0	√	6
TOTAL HOURS		22		28
TOTAL COST		£396		£252 (personal care element) + £207.90 (Direct Payments) = £459.90

Compare Typical Self Directed Assessment Decision v Typical Council Care Assessment Decision

Caring for someone—whether it's a parent, partner, or close friend—is a journey. There's no handbook, no one-size-fits-all solution, some days are smooth, and some days feel overwhelming. That's where a good care plan comes in. It's not just a checklist of tasks; it's a blueprint for making life easier, for ensuring the right support is in place before things get too chaotic. Care is about caring for another's needs. It is important to know the real needs of the person being cared for. A good care plan isn't just about schedules—it's about understanding those needs, being responsive, adapting when things change, and creating a system that brings peace of mind. It's about including activities that you normally do that could be missed out. Because when everyone is on the same page, care doesn't feel like a constant scramble. It feels like a team effort, built with love and intention.

Key Components of a Care Plan

A well-structured care plan is essential for patients transitioning from hospital to home, as it serves as a road map for ensuring comprehensive support that addresses specific needs. The key components of a care plan include a thorough assessment of individual needs, since this forms the foundation for personalised care. This assessment should include medical history, daily living requirements, mobility challenges, and any emotional or mental health considerations. Only by understanding the unique circumstances of each individual, can the caregivers tailor their services to provide the most effective support, and ensure that their clients feels secure, comfortable and cared for during their convalescence or long term care.

Another critical element of a good care plan is the identification of goals and outcomes. These goals should be realistic, measurable, and aligned with your preferences and lifestyle. For example, a goal may involve regaining the ability to perform daily tasks independently or improving mobility with the assistance of a home care worker. Establishing clear objectives not only helps in tracking progress but also empowers care users, by involving them in their care journey. Goals are important, but if you don't make a plan and get support, you are less likely to reach them.

Coordination of Care is another vital component. This means ensuring that all professionals involved in your care or recovery are on the same page. This involves creating a communications plan that outlines who is responsible for what aspects of care, including medical appointments, therapy sessions and home support services.

Regular check-ins and updates among carers, caregivers, healthcare providers, and family members are crucial for adapting the care plan as needed. By maintaining open lines of communication, potential issues can be addressed promptly; preventing setbacks and enhancing the overall care experience.

In addition to these components, the care plan should also include a detailed budget and funding options for home care services. Understanding financial assistance available for those claiming benefits such as Personal Independence Payment or Disability Living Allowance can significantly ease the burden of costs associated with home care. You should explore all available resources and funding opportunities, ensuring that they make informed decisions about their care without compromising quality. A well-planned budget allows for flexibility and ensures that the necessary support is accessible even within financial constraints.

Your care plan should prioritise your emotional and mental well-being. Especially if you are transitioning from a hospital setting to home alone, this can be daunting, and feelings of isolation or anxiety may arise. Incorporating strategies for well-being support and relaxation and planning regular social interactions and activities that promote engagement, or access to counselling services, if needed, is essential for holistic care. By addressing both physical and emotional needs, caregivers can create a supportive environment that not only aids in your recovery but also enhances the quality of life for you during your transition at home.

Steps to Develop Your Personalised Care Plan

Request a Self Directed Assessment from your local authority or relevant agency. This assessment plays a crucial role in determining the level of support you are eligible for based on your individual circumstances. Be prepared to discuss your needs openly and honestly during the assessment, as this will help the assessor understand your situation better. Remember, this is your opportunity to advocate for yourself and express what type of assistance you believe will enhance your quality of life.

To develop your personalised care plan, start by assessing your unique needs and preferences. Create a care plan using the Care Plan Assistant app. Take time to reflect on your daily activities, the challenges you face, and the support you require. Consider aspects such as mobility, personal care, medication management, and social interaction. The app will document your observations and feelings, as this foundational step will inform every part of your care plan. Collaborating with family members or friends during this process can provide additional insights and ensure that your care plan aligns with your lifestyle and values.

Preparing for a Care Needs Assessment

All adults over 18 are entitled to a local authority assessment to determine whether they qualify for financial help or care. This right is outlined in the Care Act. Adults can require care due to illness, disability, old age or poverty. However, to be eligible for care you will have to meet your local council's criteria. The criteria can be different so call your local council and find out how you can obtain a copy of their eligibility criteria, or go online to your local council website and search. All councils have to publish details of their eligibility criteria and they have a duty to make it available to local people.

Evaluating The Options

Every local authority has its own framework that it uses to assess people who met the Care Act eligibility criteria. Each assessment framework includes the initial assessment, the finalised personalised support plans, commissioning of support packages, and ongoing reviews to ensure continued alignment with your assessed needs. If you request a self-directed assessment, this means you are directing the initial assessment, the personalised support plan and dealing with some, or maybe all of the commissioning of your support package.

Once you have figure out everything you might need in your care package, write or type it out on 1 or 2 sheet of A4 paper. A Female service user, age 68, with Advance Parkinson disease, Type 2 diabetes, high blood pressure, who has social isolation issues and need to go to church and local communality centre once a week, might have a similar care plan to a 84 year old male service user, who has vascular dementia, arthritis, inflammation of the joints that can cause pain and stiffness, mild incontinence, and a neck of femur hip fracture.

Suppose we were to devise a self-direct a weekly care plan for a male service user named Tom, who is 84, has vascular dementia, arthritis, inflammation of the joints that can cause pain and stiffness, mild incontinence, and a neck of femur hip fracture. Tom needs help with personal care, washing bathing, dressing, grooming, laundry, changing the bed, heating of special meals prepared by family. Regular hydration and a cup of tea made 3 xs daily. Once weekly physiotherapy sessions, and a weekly trip to Local Park in wheelchair, help with shopping, and anti coagulant and pain medication prompting. We would read through the local authority eligibility criteria and use as many of the terms as possible. If we were to draft up an itinerary of care, we might come up with a list of care needs for Tom, similar to one below:

Weekly Care Needs for Tom (Age 84) *Service User with Vascular Dementia, Hip Fracture, Arthritis, Mild Incontinence*

Proposed Daily Care Routine
Morning:
- Assist with personal care: washing, bathing,

dressing, grooming.

- Provide support with changing the bed and handling laundry as needed.
- Serve breakfast, ensuring **hydration** (water, tea, or juice).
- Prompt **medications**, including anticoagulants and pain relief.
- Encourage gentle mobility (if safe), aiding circulation and stiffness.

Midday:

- Reheat and serve **family-prepared meals**, ensuring appropriate temperature and presentation.
- Assist with any needed hygiene tasks following meals.
- Offer **hydration** (water or tea).
- Engage in light mental stimulation (conversation, music, sensory activities).

Afternoon:

- Provide assistance with toileting, ensuring comfort and hygiene.
- Offer **hydration** (tea in afternoon).
- Engage in **gentle seated exercises** or wheelchair-supported movement.

Evening:

- Serve dinner, ensuring balance in nutrition.
- Provide further **personal care** (dressing, skin care, incontinence management).
- Ensure a **calm and soothing environment** to support relaxation.
- Final **hydration** (evening tea or water).
- Support safe transition to bed.

Weekly Activities & Support

Monday – Physiotherapy Session

- Assist with transport or in-home physiotherapy exercises.
- Gentle movement support following therapy.

Tuesday – Personal Care & Shopping Assistance

- Routine care plus **help with shopping** (escorted outing or delivered essentials).

Wednesday – Social Interaction & Relaxation

- Focus on **music, storytelling, and light engagement** at home.
- Encourage comfort-enhancing activities.

Thursday – Laundry & Domestic Support

- Dedicated **bed changing and laundry** day.
- General assistance with home environment.

Friday – Park Visit (Wheelchair Support)

- Safe, assisted trip to **Local Park** to promote well-being and sensory stimulation.

Saturday – Family Time & Meal Support

- Assist with **reheating meals**, ensuring a relaxed environment for social time.

Sunday – Relaxed Personal Care Focus

- Prioritise **comfort, hygiene, and relaxation** with minimal disruptions.

There are various types of care plans Tom might receive; based on his budget and the type of assessment he takes. Below is an example with an approximate breakdown of the daily are hours and the weekly total, along with the estimated costs that Tom would incur on what could be described as an ideal, or Optimal Plan.

The Optimal Support (47 hour) Plan.

Optimal Weekly Plan: Daily Care Breakdown

Task	Estimated Time (Hours)
Personal care (washing, dressing, grooming)	1.5
Bed changing & laundry assistance	0.5
Meal preparation & hydration assistance (3x daily)	1
Medication prompting	0.5
Mobility support & light exercises	0.5

Task	Estimated Time (Hours)
Toileting & incontinence care	0.5
Social engagement & mental stimulation	0.5
Evening care routine & transitioning to bed	1
Total per day	**6.5**

Additional Weekly Activities

Activity	Frequency	Estimated Time (Hours)
Physiotherapy session	1x/week	1
Shopping assistance	1x/week	1.5
Park visit (wheelchair support)	1x/week	1.5

Total Weekly Hours & Cost

- **Total weekly care hours: 47.5 hours**
- **Weekly cost (@£20/hour): £950**

If we break down the approximate times per day and the total hours of care in the ideal weekly care plan, we get a breakdown of how much the ideal care would cost per week, assuming the care costs were £20 per hour.

Clearly this is a high cost plan, especially if you are self funding as local councils are also requiring higher contributions to care. The local authority will usually propose a **Minimal Support Plan that** focuses on your **core care needs** while maintaining comfort, dignity, and essential well-being. Here's an approximate breakdown of the daily care hours and the weekly total, along with the estimated costs that Tom would lyrically receive on a local council Minimal **Support (15 hour) Plan.**

SEE Minimal Support (15 hour) Plan.

Minimal Support Weekly Care Plan (15 Hours)

This plan prioritises the **essential daily tasks** while streamlining non-critical support.

Daily Core Care Routine (Reduced Time)

Task	Adjusted Time (Hours)
Personal care (washing, dressing, grooming)	**0.75** (essential support only)
Meal preparation & hydration assistance (3x daily)	**0.5** (basic meal setup and hydration reminders)
Medication prompting	**0.25** (quick prompts, ensuring adherence)
Toileting & incontinence care	**0.5**
Evening care routine & transitioning to bed	**0.75**

Task	Adjusted Time (Hours)
Total per day	2.75

Weekly Activities & Support

Activity	Frequency	Adjusted Time (Hours)
Physiotherapy session	1x/week	1
Shopping assistance	1x/week	0.75 (basic errands support only)
Park visit (wheelchair support)	1x/week	1 (shortened outing)

Total Weekly Hours & Cost

- **Total weekly care hours**: 15 hours
- **Weekly cost (@£20/hour)**: **£300**

Key Adjustments for Minimal Support

- **Reduced personal care duration**, focusing on essential hygiene only.
- **Condensed meal support**, ensuring hydration and meal setup but minimising active assistance.
- **Shortened shopping & park outings**, maintaining social engagement but limiting time commitments.

- **Streamlined medication prompting**, ensuring adherence efficiently.

This plan ensures that **Tom's core needs are met while keeping costs minimal**.

A Self-Directed Assessment is ideal, because it will allow you to create a care a care and support plan that meets somewhere in the middle of **Optimal (47.5 hour)** plan and the **Minimal (15 hours)** plan. For instance, here's an approximate breakdown of the daily care hours and the weekly total, along with the estimated costs that Tom would incur on an **Optimised (25 hours) plan.** The Optimal Care Plan schedule would look a little bit like the one below:

The Optimised (25 hours) Plan

Optimised Weekly Care Plan (25 Hours)

This adjustment prioritises **essential care** while streamlining support in areas where independence or efficiency can be optimised.

Daily Care Routine (Reduced Time)

Task	Adjusted Time (Hours)
Personal care (washing, dressing, grooming)	**1** (streamlined support)
Bed changing & laundry assistance	**0.5** (twice weekly instead of daily)
Meal preparation & hydration assistance (3x	**0.5** (more efficient serving)

Task	Adjusted Time (Hours)
daily)	
Medication prompting	0.25 (streamlined prompts with routine structure)
Mobility support & light exercises	0.5
Toileting & incontinence care	0.5
Social engagement & mental stimulation	0.5
Evening care routine & transitioning to bed	0.75 (adjusted for efficiency)
Total per day	**4.5**

Weekly Activities & Support

Activity	Frequency	Adjusted Time (Hours)
Physiotherapy session	1x/week	1
Shopping assistance	1x/week	1
Park visit (wheelchair support)	1x/week	1 (shortened outing)

Total Weekly Hours & Cost

- **Total weekly care hours**: 25 hours
- **Weekly cost (@£20/hour)**: £500

Comparison of Optimal and Optimised Care Plans & Costs

Care Level	Weekly Hours	Weekly Cost (£20/hour)
Full Care Plan (Original)	47.5	£950
Optimised Care Plan (Balanced)	25	£500
Minimal Support Plan (Core Needs)	15	£300

What If I Already Have a Council Assessed Care Plan?

Minimal support care can reduce costs and maintain independence, but it does come with risks that need careful consideration. To effectively increase your care hours and improve your care, you would need to review you current care plan, you should articulate to the council why the current care plan is not meeting your needs   explain the difficulties you are having and support them with the recognised health concerns the local authority is required to address.

If you need personal care and currently only have a **Minimal Support (15 hour)** plan with your local authority, you can request a review and a self-directed assessment to improve the level of care, and up your level of care hours and services. An Adjusted Care plan can balance the Council's cost efficiency with added safeguards for things like hydration, medication adherence, mobility, and emotional well-being and create a contingency plan for flexibility—if conditions worsen, additional care should be easy to arrange. Here's an approximate breakdown of the daily care hours and the weekly total, along with the estimated costs that Tom would incur on a Council **Adjusted (20 hours)** Plan.

The Council Adjusted (20 hours) Plan

Adjusted Weekly Care Plan (20 Hours)

This plan balances efficiency with added safeguards for **hydration, medication adherence, mobility, and emotional well-being**.

Daily Care Routine (Reduced but Safer)

Task	Adjusted Time (Hours)	Risk Mitigation
Personal care (washing, dressing, grooming)	1	Ensure full hygiene routine to prevent infections.
Meal support & hydration assistance (3x daily)	0.75	Introduce **hydration reminders** or an auto-dispensing water bottle.
Medication prompting & health check	0.5	Use a **smart pill dispenser** with alerts for better adherence.
Mobility support & gentle exercises	0.5	Physiotherapist-approved **seated**

Task	Adjusted Time (Hours)	Risk Mitigation
		mobility routine daily.
Toileting & incontinence care	0.5	Regular checks to prevent discomfort.
Evening routine & transitioning to bed	0.75	Ensure safe environment with **fall-prevention measures** (sensor mats, grab rails).
Total per day	**4**	

Weekly Activities & Support (Adjusted)

Activity	Frequency	Adjusted Time (Hours)	Risk Mitigation
Physiotherapy session	1x/week	1	Ensure **home follow-up exercises** for mobility.
Shopping assistance	1x/week	1	Schedule **automated grocery deliveries** where possible.
Park visit (wheelchair support)	1x/week	1	Ensure **companion support &**

Activity	Frequency	Adjusted Time (Hours)	Risk Mitigation
			safe wheelchair use.

Total Weekly Hours & Cost

- **Total weekly care hours: 20 hours**
- **Weekly cost (@£20/hour): £400**

Additional Safety Measures

- **Wearable Emergency Alarm** – Immediate assistance in case of a fall.
- **Smart Home Adjustments** – Voice-controlled lights/heating to improve ease of use.
- **Befriending Services or Family Rotation** – Helps mitigate loneliness.
- **Structured Routine Reminders** – Dementia-friendly timers for daily tasks.

This plan **preserves independence while ensuring critical safety measures**.

If you have a minimal care plan, getting a review of your care plan can sometimes be challenging. Below are some key concerns you could raise, if you are unhappy with your current plan. All of these issues fall under the Care Act 2016 and the local authorities are required to address them.

1. Unmet Care Needs

Hygiene & Personal Care Gaps – If daily routines like washing and dressing are rushed or skipped, it could lead to skin conditions, infections, or reduced dignity.

Incontinence Management – Lack of frequent assistance might result in discomfort, irritation, or an increased risk of urinary infections.

2. Increased Health Risks

Medication Non-Adherence – With fewer care hours, missed medication prompts could lead to worsening conditions, such as blood clot risks due to missed anticoagulants.

Falls & Mobility Decline – Reduced mobility support may mean less physiotherapy, leading to stiffness, weakened muscles, and higher fall risks.

3. Social Isolation & Mental Health Impact

Limited Interaction – Minimal support may reduce opportunities for meaningful conversations, engagement, and stimulation, increasing loneliness and cognitive decline.

Emotional Well-being – A lack of consistent companionship could contribute to anxiety or depression.

4. Safety & Emergency Concerns
Delayed Help in Case of Emergencies – With fewer care hours, Tom might have longer response times to falls, accidents, or health complications.

Reduced Supervision – Dementia-related confusion or forgetfulness could lead to accidents, wandering, or mismanagement of household hazards (like forgetting to turn off appliances).

5. Strain on Family or Informal Caregivers
Higher Family Burden – If professional care is minimal, family members may need to fill gaps, potentially causing stress or burnout.

Unstructured Support – Without consistent routines, care responsibilities could become unpredictable, increasing anxiety for both Tom and caregivers.

Can You Mitigate Your Care Needs?
There are ways to supplement and mitigate the risks of minimal care. You could combine the Minimal Care with assistive technology (e.g., emergency alarms, automatic medication dispensers). You could schedule family check-ins or community support (befriending schemes, meal delivery, or neighbour visits) to ensure a structured routine to maintain hydration, mobility, and emotional support. This would be very difficult if (like many people) you find yourself without a support network.

Finalising Your Assessment

Once your assessment is completed, review the outcomes carefully. Understanding the level of support you qualify for, will guide you in selecting the right home care services and support workers. Look for resources and lists of approved providers in your area, as well as online platforms that offer reviews and ratings of home care services. This research will empower you to make informed decisions about which services best fit your needs and budget.

Finally, as you implement your personalised care plan, remain flexible and open to adjustments. Your needs may change over time, requiring updates to your care plan. Regularly check in with your caregivers and family to discuss any changes, challenges, or successes you encounter. This ongoing communication will help ensure that your care plan remains effective and supportive, and enhances your health and care journey and overall well-being. Embrace the care process as a collaborative effort, and remember that you are taking important steps towards a more independent and fulfilling life.

Reviewing and Adjusting Your Care Plan

Reviewing and adjusting your care plan is an essential step in ensuring that your home support services effectively meet your evolving needs. After being discharged from the hospital, it's common for your circumstances to change, which may necessitate revisions to your care plan. There is usually a 3 month review, followed by a 6 month, or annual review.

Periodically reviewing your plan allows you and the local authority to assess what is working well and what might require adjustment. By remaining proactive, you can ensure that you receive the appropriate level of care that supports your health and well-being.

Begin by reflecting on your current situation. Consider how well your care plan aligns with your daily needs and routines. Are there specific tasks that your support worker is handling effectively? Are there areas where you feel more assistance is needed? Gathering feedback from your caregivers, family members, or even yourself can provide valuable insights into the effectiveness of your care plan. If you keep having issues around care, regular check-ins can help identify any gaps in your care that may need addressing.

Once you and your carers have re-assessed your current situation, it's time to make necessary adjustments. This could involve requesting additional hours from your support worker or seeking specialised services if your needs have changed. If, for example, you find that you require more assistance with mobility or daily living activities, don't hesitate to communicate these issues to your care provider. They are there to support you, and making your needs known is key to receiving the best possible care.

In addition to making adjustments based on your immediate needs, it's also important to consider your long-term goals. If you are working toward greater independence or aiming to improve specific areas of your health, incorporate these aspirations into your care plan. Discuss these goals with your care and support worker, as they can help tailor their approach to support your journey effectively. This collaborative effort between you and your caregiver fosters a sense of partnership that can enhance your care experience.

Always stay informed about your rights and the resources available to you. Understanding the financial assistance options, such as Personal Independence Payment or Disability Living Allowance, NHS Continuing Healthcare, Community Nursing etc. can ease some of the financial burden associated with home care. By leveraging available resources, you can make informed decisions about your care plan that align with both your needs and your budget. If your care uses up most or your entire available budget or your care costs are capped, it makes sense to get the best care possible. Remember, reviewing and adjusting your care plan is about empowering yourself to navigate your care journey with confidence.

08

Chapter 8: Evaluating and Interviewing Home Care Workers

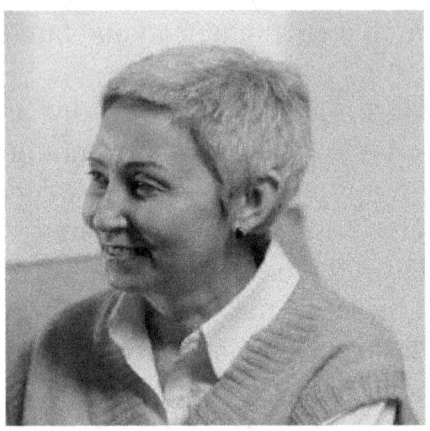

Bringing someone into your home—or into the life of someone you love—is a big deal. Care isn't just about ticking of tasks; it's about trust, connection, and making sure the right person is there to support daily life in the best way possible, is why evaluating and interviewing home care workers is so important. It's not just about finding a professional with experience—it's about finding someone who understands, listens, and respects the unique needs of the person they'll be caring for. A good match can make all the difference, turning care into comfort instead of just a service.

Imagine having a carer who is able to comb your hair the way you like it styled, cook your meals the way you like, take you out shopping, or to the park for some fresh air and physiotherapy. Would that make a difference to your health and recovery?

Where to Look for Home Care Workers

When seeking home care workers, it is essential to explore a variety of resources to find the right support tailored to your individual needs. Start by checking local agencies that specialise in home care services. Many reputable organisations provide trained professionals who can assist you with daily living activities, medication management, and companionship. These agencies often conduct the background checks for you and provide ongoing training for their staff, which can offer you peace of mind as you navigate this critical phase of recovery.

Another valuable resource is online platforms that connect caregivers with families in need of assistance. Websites and apps dedicated to home care services can help you find qualified workers in your area. These platforms often allow you to filter candidates based on specific skills, experience, and reviews from previous clients. By using online tools, you can gain access to a wider pool of potential home care workers, making it easier to find someone who meets your unique requirements.

Try the Curam Online Care Agency. It's a national care agency, which means you can find a carer in your local area. It's easy to sign up and log in, and to make contact with and interview qualified and DBS checked carers and find suitable care within hours. Find out more about choosing a carer in your area by checking out my website: www.CareCoaching.co.uk.

Also consider reaching out to local community centres, hospitals, or rehabilitation facilities for recommendations. Healthcare professionals often have connections with reliable home care workers and can provide insights into who may be best suited for your situation. Additionally, local support groups for patients recovering after surgery or long hospital stays may have valuable information and personal experiences to share, which can further guide you in your search.

Networking within your community can also yield great results. Speak with friends, family, or neighbours who may have experience hiring home care workers. Personal referrals can be incredibly helpful, as they come from service users who have first- hand knowledge of the care giver's skills and reliability.

Preparing Questions for Interviews
After identifying potential home care providers, it's essential to evaluate and interview potential support workers. Start by creating a list of questions that reflect your specific needs, such as their experience with similar cases, their approach to care, and their availability. Trust and comfort are paramount; so ensure that the caregiver aligns with your personal

values and preferences. This step not only helps you find a compatible caregiver but also fosters a sense of security as you transition back home.

Preparing questions for interviews is a crucial step in ensuring you find the right support worker for your needs. When transitioning from hospital to home, the right care can significantly impact your recovery and overall well-being. Start by considering what specific assistance you require. Are you looking for help with daily living activities, medication management, or companionship? Identifying your needs will help you formulate targeted questions that will guide your interviews with potential home care workers.

As you prepare your questions, think about the qualities that are most important to you in a caregiver. Do you value experience, empathy, or specific skills related to your condition? Tailor your questions to reflect these priorities. For example, you might ask about their previous experience with clients who have similar needs or how they approach building rapport with clients. These inquiries will not only reveal their qualifications but also provide insight into their personality and approach to care.

It's also essential to address the logistical aspects of your care. Ask the potential support workers about their availability, their flexibility with time, and how they handle emergencies. Questions such as, "How would you manage a situation where I need immediate assistance?" or "Can you accommodate changes in my schedule if my needs evolve?" will help you gauge their reliability and responsiveness. This information may be vital for establishing a care routine that aligns with your lifestyle and preferences.

Another key area to explore is the care giver's approach to communication and collaboration. Inquire about how they would involve you and your family in the care process. Questions like, "How do you communicate updates or changes in care plans?" or "What steps do you take to ensure that family members are informed and included?" will help you understand their commitment to teamwork and transparency. A caregiver who values open communication can foster a more supportive environment for your recovery.

Finally, don't hesitate to ask about their training and certifications. Look for caregivers who possess relevant certifications in health care, such as NVQs in Health and Social Care, or specialised training in areas that are pertinent to your condition. This ensures that they have the foundational knowledge necessary to provide safe and effective support. Understanding their background and qualifications can provide peace of mind and assurance that you are receiving quality care. Questions such as, "What kind of training have you completed related to my health condition?" or "Are you certified in first aid or CPR?" will help you determine their preparedness for handling various situations. By preparing thoughtful questions, you empower yourself to make informed decisions about your care, ensuring a smoother transition from hospital to home.

Best Practices for Conducting Interviews

When conducting interviews for home care worker, preparation is key. If Social services are interviewing Care Agencies or Care Contractors on your behalf, inform them you want to be present.

Write out a comprehensive list of needs that will ensure that will ensure all the essential areas are covered during the interview. Begin by outlining your specific care needs. This includes your daily routines, health conditions, and personal preferences. Consider including questions that explore the potential carer's experience, training, and approach to care, as well as scenarios they might encounter in your home setting. This preparation demonstrates your commitment to finding the right fit for your unique situation and being confident that you know exactly what you need and that you have done your research, will promote a positive atmosphere during the interview process.

During the interview, you are supposed to create a welcoming environment that encourages open communication. You should be friendly, attentive, and respectful. You should allow the candidate to share their experiences and thoughts without interruption, as this can reveal valuable insights into their personality and the type of care they offer. Using open-ended questions can facilitate a more in-depth discussion, allowing you to gauge not only their qualifications but also their empathy and compatibility with the role.

Remember, the goal is to find someone who will not only meet the technical requirements but also be there for you in a supportive and compassionate relationship.

We all like to talk about ourselves, but listening actively is the best practice that enhances the interview process. This means paying close attention to the potential care giver's responses, asking follow-up questions for clarification, and acknowledging their answers. It's important to assess not just what candidates say, but how they say it. Their demeanour and enthusiasm can be just as telling as their qualifications. Take notes during the interview to capture important points, which will be useful for comparison later. This attention to detail will reflect in your investment in finding the best care for you or your loved one

In addition to assessing the candidate's skills and personality, it's vital to discuss practical matters openly. This includes availability, flexibility, and any logistical details such as transportation or the ability to perform specific tasks. Transparency about payment and funding options is also crucial, especially for those self-funding their care. Make sure to cover any potential scheduling conflicts or special requirements that may arise. A straightforward conversation about these aspects helps set clear expectations and lays the groundwork for a successful working relationship.

Finally, if you are interviewing carers by yourself, use a reputable online agency, who vet their carers, or follow up with references and background checks after the interview process. Check out my website www,CareCoaching.co.uk for recommendations Speaking with previous employers can provide additional insights into the candidate's performance and reliability. Trust your instincts as well; if something doesn't feel right during the interview, it's worth exploring other options. Finding the right home care worker is a significant decision, and taking the time to conduct thorough interviews and evaluations can lead to a more positive experience for both the individual receiving care and their family. With patience and diligence, you can secure a supportive and trustworthy caregiver who will make a meaningful difference in your care journey.

The right support worker should not only be skilled but also compassionate, patient, and understanding. During interviews, pay attention to their communication style and how they interact with you and your family. A caregiver who listens attentively and shows genuine empathy can significantly enhance your comfort and trust, making the transition from hospital to home much smoother.

Additionally, consider checking references and reading reviews from previous clients. This can provide a clearer picture of a care giver's track record and reliability. Reliable sources, such as family members or friends who have gone through similar experiences, can also be invaluable in recommending care workers or agencies. Remember, the goal is to find someone who not only fits your practical needs but also aligns with your personal values and preferences.

Making the Final Decision

Making the final decision regarding your care plan can feel overwhelming, but it is an essential step toward ensuring your well-being and independence.
After gathering necessary information about your needs, preferences, and available resources, and conducting the self-directed assessment, you are now in a position to make informed choices. Remember, this decision is about what works best for you and your unique situation. Take your time to reflect on all the options available, as this is a crucial moment in your care journey.

Don't forget to trust your instincts when making a decision. The caregiver- client relationship is built on trust and comfort, and it's crucial that you feel confident in your choice. Take your time during the selection process, and don't rush into a decision. Your well being is paramount, and finding the right caregiver can greatly improve your recovery journey. By thoroughly assessing qualifications and experience, you're taking an important step toward creating a supportive and effective care plan tailored to your needs.

As you consider your options for home care, it's important to evaluate the various external services and support workers available to you that can provide service cheaply or for free. Also choose the caregivers who are not only qualified but also align with your personal values and preferences.

Financial considerations are also a significant part of making your final decision. Assess your budget and explore the funding options available, including potential benefits like Personal Independence Payment or Disability Living Allowance.

Understanding your financial landscape will empower you to make choices that are sustainable, effective. And allow you to feel better off overall. Additionally, you must remember to inquire about any sliding scale fees or assistance programs that may be available within your community. There are resources designed to help you navigate this often-complex financial aspect of care.

It is also crucial to consider your mental and emotional health during this transition. Post-hospital recovery can be challenging, and the right support can make a significant difference. Remember the better your recovery, the less your long term care will cost you. When selecting home care services, prioritise the agencies that emphasise mental wellness and provide companionship care, as these types of care services are essential for a holistic recovery. Engage with your support network, family, friends, or support groups, to discuss your feelings and concerns. These connections can enhance your resilience and provide additional perspectives as you make your decision.

Ultimately, making the final decision about your care plan is about ensuring you feel comfortable and empowered in your choices. Trust yourself and the process you have undertaken to arrive at this point. Remember that you have the right to advocate for your needs, and it's okay to ask for help when necessary. Then embrace the journey ahead with the confidence

09

Chapter 9: Financial Assistance and Funding Options

Let's be honest—care isn't cheap. Whether its home care, medical support, or even just the little things that make life easier, costs add up fast. And when you're already juggling responsibilities, the financial side of things can feel overwhelming. That's why good financial assistance and funding options are important. There's help out there—grants, benefits, support programs—but too many people don't realise what's available or how to access it. The right financial support can make all the difference, turning care from something stressful into something sustainable, because everyone deserves the best possible care, without the constant worry of how to afford it.

Overview of Available Financial Aid

Financial aid plays a crucial role in ensuring that care users and their families can access the necessary care services they need, especially after a hospital discharge. Various financial assistance programs are available to support those claiming Personal Independence Payment (PIP), New Style Employment and Support Allowance (ESA), and other benefits like the Armed Forces Independence Payment and Disability Living Allowance (DLA). Understanding these options can significantly alleviate the financial burden associated with securing quality home care and support services.

One of the most common forms of financial aid is the Personal Independence Payment. This benefit is designed to help cover additional costs associated with living with a disability or long-term health condition. By assessing both daily living needs and mobility requirements, PIP provides essential support that can be used to fund various care services, including hiring a home care worker. If applying, it is vital for you to provide written evidence of your care needs to ensure you receive the appropriate level of support.

Additionally, some individuals may qualify for the New Style ESA, which offers financial assistance to those who are unable to work due to health issues. This benefit can be especially beneficial for patients recovering at home post-hospitalisation, as it provides a safety net during a challenging time. It allows care users to focus on their care and treatment without the added stress of financial strain, enabling them to invest in necessary care services that promote healing and independence.

For those who may have savings exceeding £23,250 and are considering self- funding their care, exploring options such as the Constant Attendance Allowance and Pension Credit can be advantageous.

These sources of financial aid can provide additional funds to help cover care costs. It is essential to research and understand the eligibility criteria and application processes for these programs to maximise available resources effectively.

Preparing for the needs assessment
https://www.which.co.uk/reviews/later-life-care/article/care-needs- assessments/preparing-for-the-needs-assessment-a1Srf0g8OSO4

Families seeking home care services for recently discharged patients should also consider local grants and community resources that might offer financial support or subsidised services. Many organisations provide information and assistance in navigating the complexities of funding options for home care. By leveraging these resources and understanding the available financial aid, you can create a comprehensive care plan that meets unique needs while staying within budget. Remember, the health and care journey is about finding the right support, and financial aid can make the journey more manageable.

What If You Are Not Eligible For Care?

Most local authorities don't have a process for appeals for people unsatisfied with eligibility decisions. The complaints process can be used if there is no appeal pathway. Applicants can register complaints about the application process through the local authority's existing complaints procedure, addressing objections to any element of the care and support plan or related decisions.

The Care Act helps people who are not eligible for a care package. Under the Care Act, your local authority must make sure that people who live in their areas receive good services that prevent their care needs from becoming more serious, or delay the impact of their needs and that people can get access to the information and advice they need to make good decisions about care and support. The council must have a range of free ad low cost, high quality, and appropriate services to choose from.

A self-directed assessment and support even if the applicant is denied a care package, is in line with the Care Act, because being supported with good nutrition, exercise, social and outdoor activities outside of a care plan helps to improve people's independence and well-being. The Care Act makes clear that local authorities must provide or arrange services that help to prevent people from developing needs for care and support or delay people deteriorating such that they would need ongoing care and support.

If you are assessed as not eligible for a care package, ask for a referral from the Integrative Care Board for a referral to a NHS Multi Agency Safeguarding Hubs (MASHs). In order to effectively and safely manage the safeguarding aspects of referral and assessment, many regions in the UK have established "Front Door" MASHs arrangements. These teams are set up to address the needs of Adults who fell outside the Care Act duties, but are vulnerable due to domestic abuse, neglect and homelessness. The team usually coordinates with a housing officer and occupational therapist (OT), Multi Agency Safeguarding Hubs can give you help, advice and information about how to access services, and refer you to other agencies that deal with non-eligible care and support needs, that can't be access through the usual mainstream services.

Care In The Community

Beyond structured care assessments and care plans, there are additional support options that could complement or substitute formal care, depending on your needs, preferences, and available resources.

Here are a few suggestions for services that could be integrated to reduce care costs:

1. Family & Community Support

- **Family Care Rotation** – If relatives are available, tasks like meal prep, hydration checks, or companionship could be split among family members.

- **Neighbours & Local Volunteers** – Some communities have volunteer networks that provide check-ins, companionship, or basic errands.

2. Assistive Technology & Smart Devices

- **Medication Dispensers & Reminders** – Automated dispensers' help with timed medication adherence.
- **Fall Detection & Emergency Alert Devices** – Wearable sensors can call for help if a fall is detected.
- **Smart Home Adjustments** – Voice-activated lights, heating controls, and automated reminders can enhance independence.

3. Professional Support Services (Ad-Hoc or On-Demand)

- **Respite Care** – Short-term professional care, allowing family members a break.
- **Domiciliary (Home) Care Services** – Can be scheduled for specific support needs, rather than full-time care.
- **Companionship Services** – Some providers offer social interaction visits, minimising isolation.

4. Government & Charitable Resources

- **Local Authority Support** – Eligibility-based care funding or personal budget assistance.
- **Charities & Advocacy Groups** – Organisations like Age UK offer advice and practical support.
- **Community Transport Services** – Some local authorities provide wheelchair-accessible transport for outings.

5. Residential or Hybrid Care Solutions

- **Assisted Living or Extra Care Housing** – Offers independence with on-site support.
- **Day Care Centres** – Social interaction and activities in a structured setting.
- **Short-Term Rehabilitation Care** – If mobility issues require additional physiotherapy or recovery time.

Here are some **successful community support programs** that have made a meaningful impact:

1. Age UK's Befriending Services (UK)

- Provides **volunteer-led companionship** for older adults experiencing loneliness.
- Offers **phone check-ins, home visits, and social outings** to improve well-being.
- Helps reduce isolation and promotes mental health support.

2. The Men's Shed Movement (Global)

- Community-based workshops where men, particularly retirees, **engage in practical projects** like woodworking.
- Encourages **peer support, skill-sharing, and social connection** to combat loneliness.
- Originated in Australia and has expanded worldwide.

3. Timebanking UK

- A **skills-exchange system** where people trade time instead of money.
- Participants offer services (e.g., gardening, tutoring) and receive help in return.
- Strengthens **community bonds and mutual support**.

4. Shared Lives (UK)

- Matches adults needing care with **host families**, creating a home-like environment.
- Supports individuals with **learning disabilities, dementia, and mental health needs**.
- Encourages **independence and social inclusion**.

5. Food Banks and Community Fridges (UK & Global)

- Local hubs where businesses and individuals **donate surplus food**.
- Helps **reduce food waste** while supporting families in need.
- Encourages **community-led sustainability efforts**.

6. Dementia-Friendly Communities (UK & Global)

- Trains businesses, transport services, and public spaces to be **more accessible** for people with dementia.
- Provides **memory cafés, support groups, and awareness programs**.
- Helps you **stay engaged in your community**.

Finding the right home care support worker is equally essential for a smooth transition from hospital to home. Even if you are self funding. Care is not a luxury. Care is just as important to your recovery as it would be if the local authority agreed a funded care package. Having to pay for care yourself does not make it any less necessary. Keep savings or an emergency credit card for this purpose. Although you may have to cut back drastically on the amount of care, make the best care plan possible. Supplement with community services and when evaluating potential caregivers, consider their experience, adaptability, hourly cost and compatibility with your individual specific care needs. Conduct interviews with candidates to assess their understanding of the required support, the expected duration of the care arrangement and the importance of fostering a positive relationship. This step not only ensures a higher standard of care but also significantly enhances your comfort and confidence during your recovery at home.

Finally, understanding the financial aspects of care is crucial, especially for those who may have savings above the threshold for automatic funding. Exploring funding options, such as Personal Independence Payment (PIP) or Disability Living Allowance (DLA), may provide additional resources to help cover care costs.

Families should also be aware of their rights regarding home care arrangements and can still seek support from local agencies that offer guidance on navigating the processes. By taking proactive steps, you can help create an effective care plan that not only economically meets the health needs of your loved ones, but also supports their dignity and independence at home.

How to Apply for Financial Assistance
Financial assistance can play a crucial role in alleviating the burden of care costs for those navigating the complexities of health challenges. If you are claiming Personal Independence Payment (PIP), New Style Employment and Support Allowance (ESA), or

any of the other relevant benefits, applying for financial assistance can provide you with the support you need. The first step is to gather all necessary documentation, including identification, proof of income, and details about your care needs. This preparation will not only streamline the application process but also empower you to articulate your situation clearly, ensuring that your request is easy to understand and well- founded. You can find out what you are entitled to and what benefits, grants and funding you could apply for with a Benefits calculator

https://www.turn2us.org.uk/Your-Situation#A-Z

https://www.turn2us.org.uk/Get-Support

Once you have your documents ready, it's important to understand the specific eligibility criteria for each type of financial assistance. Every benefit is different. For example, the Daily Living Component of PIP and the Constant Attendance Allowance, each has its own set of guidelines that dictate who qualifies.

Research these criteria thoroughly, as this knowledge will help you tailor your application to meet the required standards. Don't hesitate to reach out to local agencies or support groups for guidance; they can offer valuable insights and support as you navigate the financial assistance landscape.

When you are ready to apply, take the time to fill out the application forms accurately and comprehensively.

Be honest and detailed in your responses, providing clear examples of how your condition affects your daily life and care needs. The **Care Plan Assistant is** an online app lets you create a plan and prepare for you assessment. You can fill out your details and generate and download a complete personalise Care Plan that can be used guides your assessment. Check out my website www.CareCoaching.co.uk for more information and free access to the app. If you still find the application process overwhelming, consider asking a trusted friend or family member for assistance. Remember, you are not alone in this journey, and having support can make the process less daunting and more manageable.

After submitting your application, be prepared for a possible assessment or review of your needs. This is an opportunity for you to present your case in person, allowing you to explain your situation in more depth. Approach your assessment with confidence, knowing that your experiences and needs are valid. It can be helpful to practice what you want to say ahead of time, ensuring you communicate your needs effectively. Additionally, keep a record of any communications related to your application, as this can be beneficial if you need to follow up or appeal a decision.

Finally, while waiting for a decision, explore other resources that may provide interim support. There are often local charities, community organisations, and online platforms that can offer assistance or advice during this time. Remember that seeking financial assistance is a proactive step towards securing the care you need. By staying informed, organised, and connected to your support system, you can navigate this process with confidence, paving the way for a smoother transition from hospital to home care.

Online Resources, Information and Tools

In today's digital age, there is a wealth of online resources available to assist individuals navigating their self-directed assessments and home care options after hospital discharge. There are websites dedicated to government benefits, such as the Personal Independence Payment (PIP) and Disability Living Allowance (DLA) that provide essential information on eligibility criteria, application processes, and the rights of patients. These platforms often include guides, FAQs, and even forums where users can share experiences and advice, making it easier for you and your family to understand the support available.

Additionally, there are various non-profit organisations and advocacy groups that focus on helping individuals with disabilities and their families. These organisations offer resources tailored to specific needs, including toolkits for requesting self-directed assessments and tips for finding suitable home care workers. Many of these groups have help lines or chat services where you can receive personalised advice, fostering a sense of community and support that can be invaluable during this transitional period.

Finding the right home care service involves careful assessment of your unique needs. Online assessment tools can guide you through identifying the level of care required, whether it's assistance with daily living activities or specialised support for chronic conditions. These tools often include questionnaires that help pinpoint specific requirements, allowing you to communicate effectively with potential caregivers. Understanding your individual needs is crucial in ensuring that you receive the appropriate support to facilitate a smooth recovery at home.

When it comes to selecting a home care worker, online platforms can aid in evaluating potential candidates. Many websites provide checklists and criteria to consider during interviews, helping you to assess qualifications, experience, and compatibility with your loved one.

Reviews and ratings from other families can also offer insight into the quality of care provided by various agencies. By leveraging these resources, you can make informed decisions that prioritise both safety and comfort in your home care arrangements.

Remember, financial assistance and funding options are critical components of securing home care services, especially for those on a budget. There are numerous online resources outline available funding sources, including grants, local council funding, and charitable organisations that offer financial support for care services. It's worth looking at what's out there.

Understanding these options can alleviate some of the financial burdens associated with care, enabling you to focus on what truly matters; the well-being and recovery of your loved one. By utilising the vast array of online resources out there, you can confidently navigate the complexities of post-hospital care and create a care plan that best suits your needs.

Budgeting for Home Care Services

Budgeting for home care services is a crucial step for those managing their health needs while navigating financial constraints. If your care costs are going to be met by personal income, such as a private pension, you want to get the most value out of your plan and consider supplementing some parts of your care with activities and services from the various specialised charities, local council services and care organisations.

If you have a very low income, where you can't meet all your care costs, there are various financial assistance options available, such as Personal Independence Payment (PIP) and Disability Living Allowance (DLA). It's essential to understand how these benefits can be effectively utilised to cover home care expenses. Begin by assessing your financial situation, including any savings and income sources, to create a realistic budget that addresses your specific needs while ensuring that you remain compliant with funding regulations.

When considering home care, it is important to identify

the level of support required. This includes not only the type of care needed, such as personal care, companionship, or assistance with daily living activities, but also the hours of care per week. In the UK, the government can potentially require you to use your home's value to fund your care costs. However, this typically happens when you move into a care home permanently and you don't have a spouse or dependent still living in your home.

Research local providers and their hourly rates, to get a sense of what the market looks like. Be sure to take advantage of free consultations offered by many agencies to discuss your needs and receive estimates. This initial stage will help you gauge potential costs and determine how far your budget can stretch while ensuring quality care.

In addition to understanding the basic costs of home care, explore available financial assistance programs to supplement your budget. You may be eligible for a range of funding. Local Authority programs and benefit calculators may provide additional resources. Investigating these options can help you to maximise your available funds and potentially reduce out-of-pocket expenses for home care services.

Once you've established your budget and explored financial assistance options use your budget as a guide when interviewing agencies and potential candidates, ensuring that you discuss the rates, services offered, and any additional fees that may arise. Building a rapport with your caregivers is essential, as they will be integral to your recovery process. Local carers may be able to offer cheaper half hour visits, or pro rate shorter calls. Trust your instincts during interviews and select someone who not only fits within your budget but also aligns with your preferences and care needs.

Finally, as you transition from hospital to home care, remember that budgeting is an ongoing process. Regularly review your expenses and adjust your budget as needed based on any changes in care requirements or financial circumstances. Open communication with your care worker about your budget can lead to flexible arrangements that meet your needs without causing financial strain. By taking these steps, you can create a sustainable plan for home care that supports your well-being and allows for a smoother recovery.

10

Chapter 10: Understanding Patient Rights in Home Care

Getting care at home should feel safe, comfortable, and respectful—but that's only possible when patients know their rights. Too often, people accept the care they're given without realising they have a say in how they're treated, who provides support, and what standards should be met. Understanding patient rights in home care isn't just about knowing the rules—it's about making sure care is truly care, not just a service. It empowers families to ask questions, demand dignity, and ensure their loved ones receive the best possible support. Everyone deserves to be treated with respect, to feel heard, and to feel they have some control.

Your Rights as a Patient

Your rights as a patient and service user are fundamental to ensuring you receive the care and support you deserve after a hospital discharge. Understanding these rights empowers you to advocate for your needs and make informed decisions regarding your care plan. As you navigate through the complexities of self-directed assessments and home care arrangements, it's vital to recognise that you have the right to receive care that is respectful, dignified, and tailored to your specific circumstances. This includes the right to participate fully in the planning of your care and to express your preferences regarding the services you receive.

You also have the right to access information about your care options. This includes details about how to request a self-directed assessment and the types of support that are available to you. Knowledge is power, and understanding what services can be included in your care plan will help you make choices that align with your goals for recovery and daily living. Whether you are seeking assistance with personal care, meal preparation, or companionship, you should feel confident in asking questions and seeking clarity about your options.

Another crucial aspect of your rights as a patient is the ability to choose your care provider. When searching for a good home care and support worker, you have the right to evaluate potential caregivers based on their qualifications, experience, and compatibility with your needs. It is important to take the time to interview candidates and discuss your expectations openly. A good caregiver will respect your preferences and work collaboratively with you to create a supportive environment that promotes your well-being and independence.

Your rights also extend to the quality of care you receive. You should expect that all services provided to you are delivered with the highest standards of professionalism and compassion. If you ever feel that the care you receive is not meeting these standards, you have the right to voice your concerns and seek changes. This may involve discussing issues with your care provider or contacting local authorities or advocacy groups that can assist you in addressing any grievances you may have.

Understanding your rights is essential not just for your physical health but also for your mental and emotional well-being. Transitioning from hospital to home can be challenging, and having an advocate—whether it's a family member, friend, or a professional—can help you navigate this process. Remember, your rights as a patient are in place to protect you and ensure that you receive the support needed for a successful recovery. Embrace this knowledge and let it guide you as you create a care plan that truly reflects your needs and aspirations.

Ensuring Your Rights Are Respected
Ensuring your rights are respected is a crucial aspect of

navigating the process of self-directed assessments and securing the care you need after a hospital discharge. Understanding your rights can empower you to advocate effectively for yourself or your loved ones. It is essential to familiarise yourself with the regulations surrounding Personal Independence Payment (PIP), New Style Employment and Support Allowance (ESA), and other financial supports available to those requiring assistance. Knowing what you are entitled to can help you approach the assessment process with confidence and clarity.

When requesting a self-directed assessment, it is vital to communicate your needs clearly and assertively. It's not just about help getting washed, dressed and fed. Be prepared to articulate the challenges you face and the kind of support that would best suit your situation. Think of the assessment like an exam, where you successfully explain to examiner your needs and how they impact on your well-being, for instance, a need for help with getting dressed or support to get to work. You discuss your health goals and the outcomes that matter to you – for example, whether you are lonely and want to make new friends This also becomes an opportunity to explain your other unique circumstances - for example, whether you are completely alone or whether you have someone gives you some support.

Remember that this is your opportunity to express how your condition affects your daily life and what assistance you require to maintain your independence. Documenting your experiences and needs can be immensely helpful during the assessment, ensuring that the professionals involved have a comprehensive understanding of your unique circumstances.

Once you have secured a self-directed assessment, the next step involves finding a suitable home care and support worker. It is your right to choose who provides your care, and you should feel empowered to make decisions that align with your preferences and requirements. Evaluating potential caregivers involves asking the right questions about their experience, approach, and understanding of your specific needs. Trust your instincts—if a caregiver does not seem like the right fit, continue your search until you find someone who meets your expectations.

It is also essential to understand that you have the right to review and adjust your care plan as your needs evolve. Life can change, and your support requirements might shift over time. Open communication with your care team allows you to express any concerns or modifications needed. Regularly reassessing your situation and advocating for necessary changes ensures that your care remains aligned with your preferences and health status, promoting a better quality of life.

Staying informed about your rights within home care arrangements is equally important. This includes understanding the grievance procedures should any issues arise with your care provider. Resources are available to help you navigate these situations, and support networks can offer guidance and advocacy. By actively ensuring your rights are respected, you foster an environment where your needs are prioritised, allowing you to focus on your recovery and well-being after your hospital discharge.

Reporting Violations and Seeking Support

Reporting violations and seeking support is a critical aspect of navigating the landscape of care and financial assistance, particularly for those claiming benefits like Personal Independence Payment (PIP) or the Disability Living Allowance (DLA). It is essential to understand that you have rights and protections under the law, and when those rights are violated, there are steps you can take to address the situation. Whether you encounter difficulties with your care provider, issues related to your benefits, or challenges in receiving the support you need, knowing how to report these violations can empower you to advocate for yourself effectively.

When you suspect that you are experiencing abuse and your rights have been compromised, the first step is to gather evidence. Phone recordings, photos and witness reports and any relevant information regarding the issue at hand. This could include documentation related to your care plan, records of communications with your care provider or local authority, and any evidence of inadequate support or services. Taking detailed notes (or having someone take them for you) will not only help you articulate your concerns better but will also serve as a reference should you need to escalate the matter. Remember that your voice matters, and by standing up for your rights, you contribute to a more equitable care environment for everyone.

Once you have compiled your information, the next step is to reach out to the local authorities safeguarding team or organisations. Age UK is a useful resource for the elderly. For more information call the Age UK Advice Line on 0800 678 1602. Age UK is open 8am to 7pm, every day of the year You can also find your local chapter by entering you post code online (https://www.ageuk.org.uk/contact-us/). Its best to report abuse claims in writing, as well as by phone.

If you have sent an email, or someone has sent a letter on your behalf to your social worker, or the care agency manager, you have a written record. For issues related to personal care services, consider contacting your local council or the Care Quality Commission (CQC), which oversees care providers in England. If your concerns are related to financial benefits, organisations such as the Department for Work and Pensions (DWP) can assist. Serious offences like assault, or theft by carers should be reported to the police and social services.

Additionally, there are advocacy groups specialising in disability rights who can provide valuable support and guidance throughout this process. Engaging with these resources can help ensure your concerns are taken seriously and addressed promptly.

Seeking support from family, friends, or community

organisations can also be incredibly beneficial. You are not alone in this journey, and having a support network can make a significant difference in navigating the complexities of care and benefits. Discuss your challenges with trusted people or services that can offer assistance or advice. They may have insights or experiences that could illuminate your path forward. Moreover, support groups and online forums can connect you with others facing similar situations, providing a sense of community and shared understanding.

Finally, remember that reporting violations and seeking support is not just about addressing your individual situation; it is about contributing to a larger movement for improved care standards and greater accountability. A lot of people are at risk of, or experiencing abuse. Every action you take helps raise awareness and can lead to positive changes in the system. Stay persistent, keep advocating for your needs, and know that your efforts are crucial in creating a more supportive and accessible environment for all those requiring care and assistance.

11

Chapter 11: Transitioning from Hospital to Home

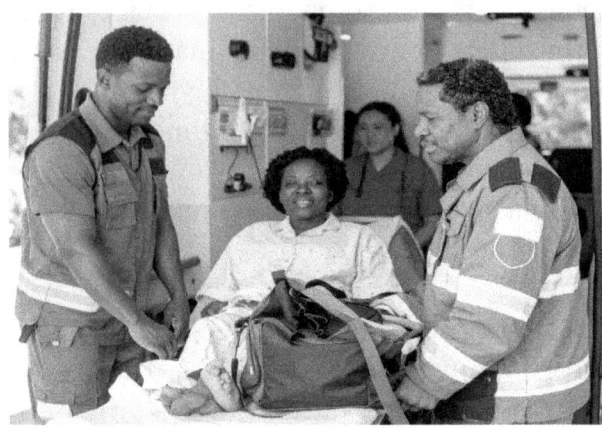

Leaving the hospital feels like a relief—but it can also be overwhelming. You may be significantly weakened from lying down for long periods of time. You may have developed new conditions, or had major surgery, you may need complex medication, may suffer from exhaustion, or need extra help with even basic tasks. Suddenly, all the support, routines, and safety nets that were in place have disappeared, and it's up to family, caregivers, and or you, to figure out what comes next? A smooth transition from hospital to home isn't just about getting back to familiar surroundings; it's about making sure recovery continues without setbacks. Whether it's managing medications, adjusting to new mobility needs, or ensuring the right care is in place, planning ahead can make all the difference.

No one should go from round-the-clock medical attention to struggling alone at home. With the right preparation (such as an Advance Statement (see Chapter 01), Healing doesn't stop at discharge—it really begins at discharge and with the right conditions, it carries on safely, comfortably, and with peace of mind.

Preparing for the Transition

Preparing for the transition from hospital to home can be a daunting process, but with the right approach, it can also be a positive step towards regaining independence and comfort. The first crucial step is to request a Self Directed Assessment. This assessment is vital, as it will evaluate all your individual needs and preferences, ensuring that the care and support you receive are tailored specifically to you. Make sure to request all available medical documents the hospital has and any information regarding your discharge plan.

In the UK, a patient who is medically fit to discharge occupies 1 in 3 hospital beds. These patients remain in hospital beds even if they don't need to due to the ongoing the lack of appropriate care equipment when they are discharged to their home. The longer a person stays in hospital in bed, the worse their morbidity, healing and recovery outcome gets. Purchasing your own disability equipment or adaptations may be a way of meeting your eligible needs and obtaining a discharge.

If you absolutely cannot afford your own mobility and

equipment, call your local council and apply for equipment for your home if you're disabled, on GOV.UK. Most people who need equipment to help them to live more independently can get it from their local authority. You can get grab bars, ramps, adaptation and disabled Facilities Grants (DFG's) This service is free, but you will need to ask for and wait for a social care needs assessment before discharge.

The NHS can loan you mobility equipment including wheelchairs and some health-related equipment, such as commodes (portable toilet), bed pans and pressure-relieving cushions and mattresses. If you have an illness or disability and cannot get the help you need from your local council or the NHS, you might be able to get a grant to help with the costs. Don't hesitate to reach out to your healthcare provider to understand the assessment process better and to discuss your specific requirements.

For more information check out the **In Control** website at: www.in-control.org.uk or to get more direct help contact In Control on Tel.: 01564 821 650, or Email: help@in-control.org.uk

Key Steps for a Smooth Transition

Understanding the key steps for a smooth transition from hospital to home can make all the difference in ensuring a successful recovery. The first step involves gathering all necessary information about the care options available to you. This includes understanding the types of assistance you may be eligible for, such as

Personal Independence Payment (PIP) or the Disability Living Allowance (DLA). Researching and familiarising yourself with these financial resources not only eases the burden of care costs but also empowers you to make informed decisions about your needs and preferences.

Once you are ready for discharge, turn your hospital bed into a home office. Consider the financial aspects of home care services. Investigate various funding options available to you, including Personal Independence Payment and other allowances. If your health or mobility has drastically changed, you may be entitled to benefits like Personal Independence Payment (PIP) or Disability Living Allowance (DLA) Understanding your financial resources will help you make informed decisions about your care plan.

Draft your Care Plan online with the Care Assistant app. Once you have initiated the Self Directed Assessment process, it's essential to focus on your finances. Once you have a clear understanding of your financial options, the crucial next step is to arrange a Self Directed Assessment. This type of assessment is designed to evaluate your individual needs and determine the level of support you require. It is essential to be thorough and honest in this assessment, as it will help identify the right resources and services tailored to your situation. Let the hospital know you are ready for discharge and prepare for the assessment by listing your current daily activities, challenges, and any specific requirements you may have, ensuring that you communicate your needs effectively.

After completing the assessment, the focus shifts to finding the right home care and support worker. You will probably need to find and interview a carer online Use a local Care Agency platform. Conduct thorough research to identify potential caregivers who specialise in post-hospital care. Finding a good home care and support worker is key. Your care worker will play a pivotal role in your recovery, so decide quickly what qualities are important to you. Do you prefer someone with experience in your specific condition, or perhaps a caregiver who shares similar interests? Creating a list of preferred skills and characteristics will help you in the evaluation process. Remember, this is about finding someone who can provide not only physical support but also companionship, which can be incredibly beneficial during your recovery.

Navigating the world of home care services can feel overwhelming, especially after a hospital discharge. If you are self-directing your care, it can be helpful to research and connect with local agencies. Look for agencies with positive reviews and a reputation for matching caregivers with clients based on their individual needs. Don't shy away from asking questions during your initial interactions. Inquire about their hiring practices, training protocols, and how they ensure the compatibility of caregivers with clients. Prioritise the carers and agencies that specialise in post-hospital care and have experience with patients in similar situations. This proactive approach will give you confidence in your ability to cope with your care.

When interviewing potential acute care workers, be sure to assess not only their experience but also their interpersonal skills. Take the time to ensure they understand your specific needs and preferences. It's okay to be selective; this person will be an integral part of your daily life, and establishing trust is key to a successful caregiver relationship. Care is personal. It's not discrimination to want a person you are comfortable with. A good caregiver should be patient, empathetic, and able to communicate effectively. Prepare a list of questions that address your specific needs, such as their approach to managing daily tasks, handling emergencies, and supporting mental health during your recovery. Trust your instincts during these interviews; the right caregiver will resonate with you and make you feel at ease.

Remember, you are not alone in this journey. Reach out to family, friends, or support groups who can assist you in navigating these transitions. There are numerous resources available to provide guidance and assistance, ensuring that your transition is smooth and that your care needs are met effectively. By preparing thoughtfully and surrounding yourself with the right support, you can create the right care plan that not only meets your needs but also promotes your overall well-being as you transition through life.

What is Reablement Services?
Another great reason to request a "Self-Directed"

assessment is the NHS Reablement Team support. Not all types of care and support services involves a cost for the user/ The Care Act only gives local authorities the power to charge for care and support services, they may not charge for services which the regulations say must always be free, for example Reablement services, equipment and minor adaptations to the home are free.

The NHS Reablement Team services can help adults regain their independence and ability to undertake their personal care for themselves without relying on care services. These services assist people who are struggling with daily tasks around the home. This includes tasks such as cooking, washing, dressing, or getting to the toilet.

Reablement services were created to help people regain their independence so that they would not need long term care or would have reduced care needs and ongoing support from external care services. Strategic Reablement support can drastically reduce the costs of your care costs.

Having temporary care at home can be helpful after major surgery, hip fractures, or issues like dementia and arthritis, physiotherapy, supplementation, a change in diet and lifestyle and short-term support. They can help and support you to regain your confidence and ability to easily do everyday tasks by yourself. By contrast, home care is generally provided, on the basis the service user never regains their independence and will always be reliant on home care services.

Put your search engine to work. Don't hesitate to reach out to local support groups or online forums for recommendations for care agencies or independent care. This initial groundwork will help you feel more confident in your choices and ensure that your selected caregiver aligns with your preferences and values.

Evaluating and interviewing potential home care workers is a vital step in the transition process. You can initially find a carer, while you are a patient in hospital, by going online and enrolling in an online care agency, where Interviews can be conducted by video call while you are in hospital. Based on your income, part or all of costs of your home care can be reimbursed if you are discharged from hospital and it is determined that you are eligible for NHS Continuing Care, or a Council funded care package. During the phone and video conferencing interviews, ask potential carers about their experience, qualifications, and approach to caregiving. It's important to discuss your specific needs and expectations openly. Trust your instincts; a care giver's personality and demeanour can significantly impact your comfort and recovery at home. Don't feel pressured to take the first available carer. Ensure that you feel a connection with the person who will be assisting you.

Staying organised and proactive throughout the transition will enhance your overall experience. Once you are back home, keep all your documents, discharge info, assessments, and contact information in one place for easy access. Regularly check-in with your caregiver and continue to communicate openly about your needs as they may evolve over time. Don't forget to seek support for your mental health during this period. Hospitalisation can be very traumatic and arranging your own care, discharge and transitioning home can be mentally, physically and emotionally challenging. It's easy to get depressed. Emphasising your mental well-being will facilitate a smoother recovery and foster a positive atmosphere in your home.

Ongoing Support During the Transition
Ongoing support during the transition from hospital to home is crucial. This phase is also challenging as it involves not only physical recovery but also emotional and financial adjustments.

One of the first steps in ensuring ongoing support is to establish a clear line of communication with healthcare providers. After being discharged, maintaining written contact with your medical team will allow for ongoing evaluations of your health condition and any required adjustments to your care plan. Don't hesitate to reach out with written questions or concerns. Regular check-ins helps you feel secure and informed, and makes it easier to amend your care plan.

Additionally, your family and friends can play an invaluable role during this transitional period. Your loved ones not only provide emotional support but they can assist in managing daily tasks that would feel overwhelming at first. Encourage family and friends to participate in your care plan discussions and explore ways they can contribute, whether that's helping with household chores or simply being there to listen. This collaborative approach can foster a sense of concerned, community and belonging, essential for recovery.

Finally, there are financial assistance options, that are available, that can help ease the burden of care costs. The time spent investigating various funding sources, including government benefits and local community resources, should be considered and investment. Since many organisations offer support and services that can save you hundreds off your weekly care plan and offer a chance for outdoor travel or social activities. Many organisations offer grants, respite options or subsidised services that can help you and your family manage your expenses while receiving the necessary support.

It's great to have friends and family around to support you. You may be using this book for self help and support. More and more often, people are finding that they are alone without help when navigating their care. Navigating care on your own requires an extra level of toughness, but it can be done. Understanding your rights and properly navigating all the available resources will empower you to advocate for yourself and the care you deserve. With the right support in place, transitioning from hospital to home, or moving strategically from being completely independent to needing support can be a positive experience, paving the way for a new life and new ways of thinking.

Chapter 12: Supporting Mental Health During Recovery

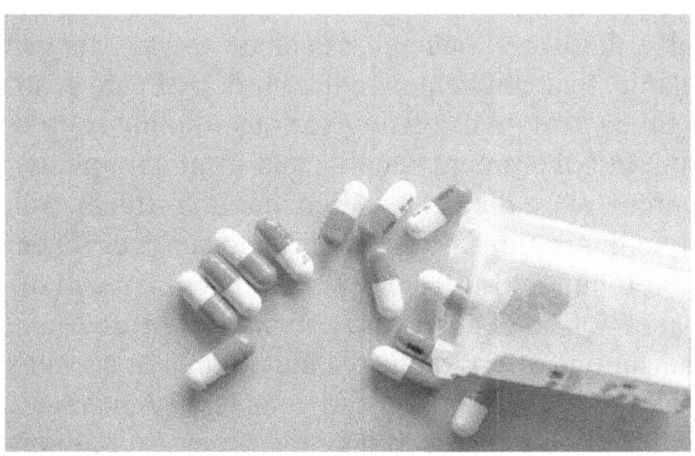

Recovering from a major illness or trauma isn't just about physical healing—it's about finding a way back to you. The body might be on the mend, but the mind often lags behind, weighed down by fear, frustration, or the sheer exhaustion of what's been endured. That's why supporting mental health during recovery is just as important as managing medications or physical therapy. No one should have to carry his or her emotional burdens alone. With the right support—whether it's therapy, open conversations, or even small daily moments of reassurance—healing becomes more than just survival. It becomes strength, resilience, and the ability to move forward with hope.

Recognising Mental Health Needs Post-Discharge

Identifying the signs that someone may need additional mental health support is vital. Family members and caregivers might be observant about changes in your behaviour, mood swings, or a decrease in interest in activities you once enjoyed. Open conversations about feelings can help reduce stigma and encourage people to express their concerns. Additionally, regular talking therapy, if done with sensitivity, can help to create a supportive environment where your feelings can be discussed freely and without judgment.

Recognising mental health needs post- discharge is a crucial step in ensuring a smooth transition from hospital to home. After a long or traumatic hospital stay, many patients may experience a range of emotional responses, including anxiety, depression, or feelings of isolation. These feelings are normal but can be exacerbated by the sudden shift from a structured environment to the challenges of daily life. It is essential to acknowledge these mental health needs such as depression and take proactive steps to address them as part of a comprehensive care plan.

Often it can be beneficial to integrate mental health care and resources into your care plan. Establish connections with local mental health professionals, support groups, or community services that can provide support or assistance. Organisations like Mind offer specialised programs for patients transitioning from hospital care, which can include therapy sessions, counselling, or peer support. These resources might be helpful in providing the emotional support.

Mind: https://www.mind.org.uk/information-support/types-of-mental-health- problems/mental-health-problems-introduction/support-services/

Sometimes mental health needs are related to isolation and neglect. Supportive families and caregivers will encourage you to engage in enjoyable activities, and promote a balanced routine, and facilitate social connections, which can contribute to improving mental health outcomes. Additionally, learning about common mental health issues associated with post-discharge recovery can empower your caregivers to recognise when a professional intervention may be necessary.

Resources for Mental Health Support at Home
Navigating the transition from hospital to home can be both a relief and a challenge, particularly when it comes to mental health. It is essential to recognise that emotional well-being plays a crucial role in recovery.

There are a number of resources available to support mental health at home, starting with community services. Local mental health organisations often provide helplines, support groups, and counselling services that can be accessed from the comfort of your home. Some of these services are useful in helping people cope with anxiety, depression, or loneliness that can arise after a hospital stay, or if you have a pre-existing mental health condition.

Online platforms also offer a wealth of mental health support options. There are many websites, YouTube videos and applications dedicated to mental wellness that provide guided meditation, stress management techniques, and cognitive behavioural therapy exercises that can be practised at home. Many of these resources are free or low-cost, making them accessible for those on a budget. Engaging with these digital tools can help you to develop coping strategies and foster a sense of control over your mental health journey.

It's also beneficial to explore social support networks. Family and friends can be a source of comfort, but sometimes additional help is needed.

Online forums and community groups focused on mental health can create a sense of belonging and provide a space to share experiences. Connecting with others who understand the challenges of recovery can reduce feelings of isolation and promote emotional resilience. Encouraging loved ones to participate in these discussions can also strengthen relationships and foster a supportive environment at home.

Private professional help should not be overlooked. Integrated Health doctors can prescribe herbal remedies like Saint John's Wort and other natural antidepressants, that don't interact with prescriptions medication. Many counsellors offer virtual sessions, making it easier to access mental health support without the need for travel. If in- person visits are more suitable, local mental health clinics often have sliding scale fees to accommodate those with financial constraints. It is important to seek out professionals who specialise in post-hospital recovery and can tailor their approach to your individual needs. Build a relationship with counselling services that provide ongoing support and guidance for these types of critical transition periods.

Patients transitioning from the Mental Health Services need extra care and support. NHS community mental health services play a crucial role in delivering mental health care for adults and older adults with severe mental health needs as close to home as possible. The Community Mental Health Framework (CMHF) replaced the Care Programme Approach (CPA) for community mental health services. CMHF enables services to shift away from an inequitable, rigid and arbitrary CPA classification and brings up the standard of care towards a minimum universal standard, and expectation of high-quality care for everyone in need of community mental health-related care. The NHS long term plan and NHS mental health implementation plan for 2019/20 – 2023/24 set out that the NHS will develop new and integrated models of primary and community mental health care. This new community-based offer should include access to psychological therapies, improved physical health care, employment support, personalised and trauma informed care, medicines management and support for self-harm and coexisting substance use.

The new NHS community-based mental health services plan is supposed to enable at least 370,000 adults and older adults per year nationally to have greater choice and control over their care, and to live well in their communities. Find out more about the service on the link below.

NHS community mental health services information: https://www.england.nhs.uk/mental-health/adults/cmhs/

Self-care practices are essential to maintaining mental health at home. Simple activities such as journaling, engaging in hobbies, natural remedies or practising mindfulness can significantly improve emotional well-being. Establishing a daily routine that includes time for relaxation and self-reflection can create a sense of normalcy and stability. Encouraging people to prioritise their mental health and incorporate enjoyable activities into their daily lives is crucial for fostering resilience and promoting a positive care or recovery experience.

NeuroLaunch offers Step Down Programs:
For Instance, NeuroLaunch offers Step Down Programs in Mental Health help with transitioning to independence with support. The NeuroLaunch step down programs are sort of mental health boot camp, but with less yelling and more compassion.

These programs are designed to ease the transition

patients from mental health to community-based support, offering a middle ground where patients can continue to receive professional help while also dipping their toes back into the waters of everyday life. NeuroLaunch have a detailed website which you can explore on the link below.

NeuroLaunch: https://neurolaunch.com/step-down-program-mental-health/

Strategies for Caregivers to Support Mental Well-Being

There are strategies for caregivers to support mental well-being focus on fostering an environment that prioritises emotional health while navigating the challenges of post-hospital recovery. Caregivers can play a pivotal role in recovery by establishing open lines of communication, ensuring that their clients feel heard and understood. Regular check-ins about feelings and concerns can help address any anxiety or sadness that may arise during the care transition. Your carer should always encourage you to calmly express your emotions and fears and create a supportive atmosphere that makes you feel less isolated.

Implementing daily routines can significantly enhance mental your well-being. Your caregiver should work with you to develop a structured schedule that includes time for meals, medication, and recreational activities. Integrating enjoyable activities, such as reading to you, crafting, or gentle exercise, can help provide a sense of normalcy and purpose. Set routines can also help to you to reduce feelings of uncertainty and stress, which contributes to a more stable emotional environment. By encouraging participation in familiar and enjoyable tasks, caregivers can help you feel more in control and engaged in your recovery process.

Getting out and about in the fresh air, social interaction and the feeling of being really listened to, is another critical component of mental health. Caregivers should encourage you to make more connections with family and friends, whether through in-person visits, phone calls, or virtual meetings. Engaging with loved ones regarding care can combat feelings of loneliness and helps people feel wanted.

Additionally, caregivers can explore local community groups or support networks that align with your interests. Participation in different activities can provide not only emotional support but also offer valuable opportunities to build new friendships and connections, enhancing overall mental well-being. Activities that incorporate mindfulness and relaxation techniques like art classes can also be beneficial for your mental health during aftercare and recovery.

Good caregivers can introduce practices such as deep breathing exercises, meditation, or gentle yoga to help reduce stress and anxiety. These activities can promote a sense of calm and help you focus on the present moment, which is especially useful when coping with the challenges of recovery. Encouraging participation in these practices together can also strengthen the caregiver-client bond.

If possible, recognising and addressing family in mental health needs post hospital discharge is an essential component of a successful recovery plan. By being proactive, utilising available resources, and fostering open dialogues about depression and mental health, family, loved ones and carers can significantly enhance your transition back home. This approach promotes a holistic view of health that encompasses both physical and mental well-being, ultimately leading to a more fulfilling and independent life.

Your family and caregivers should watch out for signs of mental health struggles and be ready to help you seek support, if needed. It doesn't just have to be about professional services, it could be a hug. Understanding that recovery is not just about physical healing but also emotional resilience is crucial. Your family should help you to attend church, find a therapist you like, or find you other spiritual or well-being practices. They should be informed about available mental health resources, including support groups and counselling services, check the reviews and encourage you to utilise these services when appropriate. By being proactive and attentive, caregivers can ensure that they are supporting you and that you receive the comprehensive care you need to thrive, both physically and mentally, during your recovery journey.

More Useful Links:
The Help and Advice, free, eBook, which has 101

brilliant ways to save money:
https://helpandadvice.co.uk/101-money-saving-tips-download/

Family Trusts: Do family trusts work? How can they protect my family, home and wealth?
https://willassociates.co.uk/services/living-trusts

You could get **Carer's Allowance** if you care for someone at least 35 hours a week and they get certain benefits. You do not have to be related to, or live with them https://www.gov.uk/carers-allowance/eligibility

Personal Independence Payment (PIP) replaces Disability Living Allowance (DLA) - Find out about how and when to claim, rates, eligibility.
https://www.gov.uk/pip

Attendance Allowance helps pay for your personal care if you've reached State Pension age and are disabled -
https://www.gov.uk/attendance-allowance/eligibility

Shared Lives scheme information:
https://www.scie.org.uk/housing/role-of-housing/promising- practice/models/shared-lives

In Conclusion

The UK care system is in crisis. Many families have complained to the Health Service Ombudsman and the CQC about care service quality and regional and post code care disparities. The UK care system is currently feared and felt of, as the end of the road. I work as a care consultant and aside from occasional praise for one of or two exemplary carers, l often listen to complaints from clients and families about council commissioned care. There are complaints about carers coming late, handling clients roughly, asking for money, stealing, not turning up, making false reports about access, not knocking on doors and barging in, not tidying up, not staying for the agreed time periods, forcing medication, physically abusing clients, not washing clients properly, not washing their hands, not able to work with the client's hair texture, who are only willing to throw a ready meal in the microwave. Carers not speaking in English, not turning off the TV, lights, appliances, or closing the curtains, not turning on the heating in winter, not locking doors, or double locking clients in when they leave and issues with multiple carers, coming and going, at different times of the day. Carers are overworked and under paid. When you consider it all, it's no wonder so many people do not thrive when they go into the care system.

When you are self-directing, care does not have to mean the end of the road. A good care plan, proper organisation can change your finances, service choices, and entire care experience. I hope this is the case for you and that this book becomes a helpful resource.

www.ingramcontent.com/pod-product-compliance
Lightning Source LLC
LaVergne TN
LVHW051049080426
835508LV00019B/1781